CANCER & PEACE, MY 15-YEAR JOURNEY

How I Found Comfort & Joy

by

Peter A. Scalzo

WWW.OAKLEAPRESS.COM

DEDICATION

The desire of my heart is to leave a legacy for my children and for them to have an understanding of how I find meaning and purpose in my life journey, especially in the face of difficulty. I dedicate this book to my children: Hilary Joy, Chelsea Hope, Paul Andrew, Spencer Andrew, Pearl Elizabeth, and Heather Marie.

ACKNOWLEDGEMENTS

There are too many people to acknowledge as they have played such an essential role in my journey. So many people have partnered with me. I am so grateful for everyone. My immediate family has had to live through each ebb and flow of my journey. I am sorry that it has been such a difficult and arduous journey. I can't believe how blessed I have been: I have not spent one night alone in the hospital since 2015. One of my children has always been with me—it brings tears to my eyes. My family has helped me in every way possible. I think my brother Paul has learned way more medical things than he ever wanted to know. He is always there for me. I have had a church community that has supported and prayed for me. I have had extended family, friends, pastors, churches, law colleagues and people I barely knew: praying, calling, sending messages and cards, driving me to appointments, making meals and generally loving on me and my family. I have had friends like Johnny D, Richard M and David S go above and beyond. I have had such great support from the cancer support group and CR forever family. I am a blessed man. I have had such wonderful medical support, and I recognize them in Chapter Seven of this book. I would like to give a special mention to Dr. Michael Grasso who won't give up on me. I also want to recognize our little poodle named Sophie who had a sixth sense about my cancer struggle and was a comforter of the highest order. For the writing of this book, I would like to thank Stephen Hawley Martin as my editor and publisher. Above all, I acknowledge my Higher Power, Jesus Christ.

CONTENTS

"Destiny itself is like a wonderful wide tapestry in which every thread is guided by an unspeakable tender hand, placed beside another thread and held and carried by a hundred others."

— Rainer Maria Rilke [1875-1926]

Introduction

I did not want to write this book. I didn't feel the desire, the energy, nor did I feel a passion for it. Frankly, I want to distance myself from cancer in any way I can, whenever I can, and I definitely do not want to be defined by cancer. I would much prefer to function as a typical guy—working, loving, and playing. But that's not how things have worked out.

I was at an evening gala for a local faith-based charity about six months ago when the unimaginable happened—three people approached me out of the blue asking for a copy of my book.

I thought, "What book?"

This wasn't the first time. People had asked me before to write a book about my journey into cancer, and I had politely said, "Maybe some day."

Then a local pastor, who had heard me speak once, approached me at the same event with the dreaded "God card."

"God told me to tell you to write a book," he said.

You gotta be kidding me, I thought. But I had heard the message, and that night I made a decision to heed God's call and get going on the book.

Let me be very clear about what you will find in the coming pages: I have a relationship with my Higher Power. My cancer journey has been as much a spiritual and emotional journey as it has been a physical one. I am in my 15th year on this trip—that's how long it's been since my first major surgery. I've had more than 15 surgeries, and that's not counting procedures, countless tests, more than 40 immunotherapy infusions, chemo rinses, five weeks of radiation therapy and six recurrences.

My NYC doctors are amazed that I'm still alive.

My Higher Power is Jesus Christ. At times, I have had to wrestle with my faith in God because of the cancer and the prospect of dying. It has not been easy. Along the way, I have made decisions, as I felt led by God, to plant myself in certain camps of spiritual understanding as you will see.

This book is not meant by any means to be a theology of suffering. It is not meant to explain how a loving God—as I understand Him to be—can allow someone like me or you to experience pain and suffering. I certainly don't understand all of it, and I doubt I ever will. I know that I live in a broken body in a broken world. What this book does attempt to explain is how I survive, and how at times I am actually able to thrive—even in the midst of the world of cancer.

I would like to express my deepest gratitude to my family—to all of you—friends, forever family, community, law partners and finally my local church. It would be so very prideful and wrong to say that I am on this journey without you. That is not the case.

In many ways, I have been a failure. I have often defaulted to fear, anxiety, worry, and anger. If having a relationship with a Higher Power is a crutch, then thank God for my crutch. God has provided comfort when there was none, joy when there should not have been joy, courage when things looked hopeless, and an utter peace that I cannot adequately explain in words.

I can tell you that I do believe in heaven. Twice the advice has been to go home and call hospice. My belief in a place called heaven has been my exit strategy. It has been a hope that does not, and I believe will not, disappoint.

God has turned my mourning into joy. Many times I have been told that I walk in peace despite my circumstances. It is not me that generates the peace. It is the God of peace in me.

I could go on and on but I will not. If you are interested, please read this book and enjoy this book. It is a glimpse into my life and where I have been walking for the last 15 years. I am not defined by cancer, but cancer has given me the platform that God wanted me to have so that He could speak to me, and to others—perhaps including you.

I am still on the journey, and I do not know where it is going or how it will end. My mantra is two words: "surrender and trust."

In 2 Corinthians 1:3-4 (NIV), the Apostle Paul writes, "Praise be to the God and Father of our Lord Jesus Christ, the Father of compassion and the God of all comfort, who comforts us in all our troubles, so that we can comfort those in any trouble with the comfort we ourselves receive from God." That's true. I have a desire to comfort others with the same comfort that I received and to encourage others in their life's journeys. To encourage means to put courage in. I pray that you will find comfort and encouragement in the pages of this book and in my life journey.

Thank you.

Chapter One
My World Before Cancer

No doubt about it, life is messy and often hard to take. It may not start out that way for most people, but I'm willing to bet almost anything that practically no one makes it from birth all the way to death without some serious troubles along the way.

That may be why you're reading this book. You or a loved one may have cancer, you may recently have had a death in the family, or you could be dealing with a divorce, addiction, or bankruptcy. Let me tell you something I know for sure: there is help. If there were not, I wouldn't be writing this book. Right now, at this moment in time you may not believe it, but a Higher Power exists that you can latch onto—cling to through the raging storms that disrupt your life. I'm going to explain how I found it, and how without that relationship, I would not be alive today, and at the keyboard typing these words. I have come to believe that finding and forming a relationship with this Higher Power is the primary reason you and I were born. Nothing—absolutely nothing—is more important.

I believed in a Higher Power from an early age—felt the presence of what I now know as the Holy Sprit in my life as a young child—but a fuller revelation of it came at age ten when all of a sudden—at least it seemed that way to my ten year old mind—my family found itself attending a Southern Baptist church in Danbury, Connecticut. Think about that. Danbury Connecticut is perhaps one of the most improbable places on earth to find a Southern Baptist Church, and my family was not from the South. My dad's folks had come from Italy through Ellis Island a couple of generations back. He had been raised as a Roman Catholic. My mother was an Episcopalian. But, as the saying goes, "God works in mysterious ways."

You see, my oldest sister had been on a spiritual journey, and my parents were curious about what was going on with her. So they invited the pastor of her church to come to our house. Once in our living room, he handed my mom and dad each a piece of paper and a pencil.

"Write down all your sins," he said. "Everything in your life you've done wrong."

They did as they were told.

The preacher then explained that by accepting Jesus as Lord and Savior, those sins would be washed away. The pastor said that was so because of Jesus' sacrifice on the Cross.

As the evening progressed, the preacher introduced my mom and dad to a personal relationship with Christ that up until that day they had not known was possible. Nevertheless, when he left, my dad balled up his piece of paper and threw it in the trash. My mother tried to retrieve it, but my dad saw her. Amused that she wanted to know what he'd written, he persuaded her to give him the ball of paper and then ripped it to shreds.

Mom and Dad went to bed that night and slept soundly—for a while. At about three o'clock in the morning, they both woke up, sat up in bed, and looked at each other.

"It's true," they said, simultaneously.

After that our household set out on a completely new tack. My dad became what you might call a "Christian-holic." There always seemed to be men in our house he was discipling, summer missionaries would stay in our house, and my mom and dad attended Bible studies as often as they could. You might say, our home became Evangelical Christian Grand Central.

At age ten, I walked down the aisle, went to the altar, and accepted Jesus as Lord. I can tell you, I was full of peace and joy that day. I knew Jesus was the Christ—God incarnate—I knew it in my heart. But there were other days when I wasn't quite so enthusiastic. The truth is I felt somewhat conflicted, and I suppose I felt a little resentful, particularly during my teenage years, that we spent practically all day every Sunday at church, as well as every Wednesday evening. And that's not to mention all the Christian activities in between at Evangelical Christian Grand Central, our home.

Let me tell you a bit more about me so that you will understand how I reacted as I did when I came face to face for the first time with cancer. I am the youngest of four children and was the "baby" of the family, especially for Mom. She babied me until the day she died. When I was very young, I was labeled the "sensitive one" by my Dad, and I believe it was true. I definitely did not have a thick skin and allowed what others thought about me to rule my thoughts about myself. I was easily hurt by others and cried easily. For most of my life, I did not understand the concept of healthy boundaries in order to have a healthy concept about myself. I became a people pleaser, and when my feelings were affected, I suppressed them. I would not allow myself to outwardly express most feelings or emotions. I viewed emotions, especially crying, as weak. As an emotional person, I was definitely unhealthy and bottled up. This absolutely had a negative impact on me and others as I entered into my cancer journey.

One thing I learned from my dad was that hard work and performance are to be highly valued. Whenever he, my uncle, and my grandfather talked about someone at work during a holiday dinner, for example, they would say things like, "Joe Jones is a good man. He's a hard worker." That's how they were. Getting a job done well was extremely important to them. My dad was born during the depression and had a tremendously strong work ethic. He ran the family retail appliance business and worked long hours—often ten hours a day, six days a week. At the outset of Mom and Dad's marriage, he told her, "You take care of the kids, and I'll bring home the money." And so, with his work and his Christian activities, he didn't have time for much of anything else. He was an excellent provider, but I can only recall him attending a handful of school events and athletic contests over the years. I think this affected my relationship with Dad. With my inability to genuinely communicate my feelings to him, and my penchant for people pleasing, I did not open up to him about many issues I was facing as I was growing up. I felt as though there was an invisible barrier between us.

My mother, on the other hand, did what she could to fill the gap. She was my go-to person. I felt safe with her. I could tell her anything, and did.

"This is my baby," she would say when introducing me—even when I was a grown man. I sincerely believe that if I had come home after robbing a bank, she would have brought me some milk and cookies, and said in a soft and genuinely curious voice, "How did the bank robbery go?"

Most of my friends were Catholics, and at fourteen, I enrolled in a Catholic high school. There weren't many of what I would call evangelical Christians my age—hardly any at all. Looking back, I will say that I was a pretty good kid, and most people liked me. Even though I was inwardly unsure of myself, I was outgoing and friendly. I suppose because of feelings of insecurity—because of my low sense of self worth—I became a people pleaser, hoping that by pleasing others, they would like me, and I guess for the most part, they did. But deep down, I harbored an unspoken sense of loneliness. I longed for spiritual connections, deep connections, with people my age who shared my evangelical Christian beliefs. I had a very close friend named Peter, who remains a close friend today, but he was not on the same spiritual journey. What I longed for were friends and companions who read the Bible and attended Christian concerts—that sort of thing. And more than anything else, I wanted a girlfriend who shared those beliefs. I remember crying out to the Lord, saying, "Lord, I would really love to have more connections, spiritually, and I would love to have a girlfriend."

Around that time, a speaker came to our church to talk about prayer, and the thing that struck me about what he said was that we ought to pray specifically for what we want. So I prayed, "Lord, I want a Christian girlfriend I can connect with spiritually, and have fun with. Oh, and by the way, Lord, I want her to be blond, beautiful, and about 5'9" tall."

About that same time, my mom kept telling me there was a girl at Church she wanted me to meet, but I wasn't so sure I wanted to meet a girl my mom had picked out for me. Nevertheless, the next time we were at Church, my mom spotted her.

"There she is," my mom said. "That's the young woman I want you to meet."

The young woman spotted my mom and found her way to us.

It was unbelievable. There she was, the spot-on answer to my prayer—beautiful, blond, 5'9" tall, an evangelical Christian—my future wife, Leslie. Southern Baptists, her parents had moved to the area from Texas because her father was an airline pilot that flew out of the New York airports. Not only was she a beauty, she was well-liked at her school, Newtown High, and not surprisingly was the reigning Homecoming Queen. Our first date was to attend a Bible study being taught at our Church by my father.

I have to admit, I was very shy around her. There was I—with my low sense of self worth—dating a homecoming queen. But I was definitely motivated to make it work and forced myself to move ahead with the relationship. We would talk every day on the phone. We went on dates, and we connected most of all, I believe, because we both were evangelical Christians in a part of the world where there weren't many others our age.

When we were about 18, Leslie and I went together to a Christian camp called "Agape Farm," in Pennsylvania. There were hundreds of people camping, as well as Christian artists playing Christian music, and of course, there were Christian speakers. I recall seeing people raising hands and praising the Lord. It was quite a sight, but I guess I'd lost some of my enthusiasm for Jesus over the years because I thought to myself, "I just can't do that. I would be a fraud—I don't feel that way."

Those thoughts must have had a big effect on me because driving home, I recall that I started to weep. At first I couldn't quite figure out why. What was wrong with me? Then it hit me. It was because of the Lord. I was having an experience with Him. I realized I wanted to surrender my life to Jesus. I said, "I want You to be number one in my life, Lord, but I need to know that you are real. If I'm going to surrender to you, I must know that you are real."

We arrived at my parents' driveway, and I turned the car in and brought it to a stop. Leslie took my hand, and I experienced the power of the Lord in an extraordinary and tangible way. I couldn't move—was paralyzed. I said to myself, "Move!" but I simply could not. My heart was racing, and I experienced the presence of the Holy Spirit. I'd asked Jesus to show me He was real, and He did show me. He showed me right there in my parents' driveway with Leslie holding my hand.

From that moment forward, I had an unabiding hunger for the Scriptures and a hunger for the Lord.

Leslie and I were joined at the hip in those days. We went steady in high school, and then we both went off to college. I studied business and Bible at Messiah College in central Pennsylvania—Bible because I wanted to learn as much as possible about the Scriptures, and business because it was understood that I would go to work in the family firm.

Leslie went to Gordon, a Christian college in Wenham, Massachusetts, and it was difficult being apart. We told each other we could date others, and Leslie did try that a few times. But we always came back to one another, and so perhaps it's not surprising that we were married just after my junior year. Our first home was an apartment in the basement of a professor's house.

After my graduation in 1984, we packed up the car and headed back to Connecticut. That was on a Saturday, and I was to begin work in the family business, Scalzo Appliances, the following Monday morning. My dad was anxious for me to manage the retail side of business and thereby take some of the burden off him. So he handed it over the very first day. I was 22 years old and had graduated college less than 48 hours prior to being given that responsibility.

Leslie and I lived in my parents' house at first. But after a few years, we had a house of our own built on a beautiful spot—a colonial style house—and began having children. I must confess, however, that I was not happy in my job. As you will recall, I was a people pleaser, and it didn't take long for people—employees and customers—to figure that out. It's very hard to run a retail business with forty or so employees, and customers that inevitably have complaints, when you have difficulty saying the word, "no," and besides that—perhaps even more important—I simply did not find selling appliances to be interesting or a satisfying way to spend my life. Imagine the anxiety it caused.

The stress I was under often made me physically ill. My doctors could find nothing physically wrong, but my symptoms were very real. My gut was in constant turmoil. About once a month I'd spend an entire weekend throwing up. It was clear I was not in the right business, but I was conflicted about leaving it because I felt a sense of allegiance to my dad. He'd worked fifty years in the business, had finally reached a point when he could turn it over to someone, and that someone was me. I didn't want to let him down.

Nevertheless, I prayed to the Lord, "Lord, I want out. I just want out. Please find a way. My dad is a God fearing man, God. Please talk to him. Whisper in his ear. Find me a way out."

I knew I needed to do something, but I didn't know what. I thought, *Perhaps it's to go back to school.* But I couldn't put my finger on what I wanted to study—what I wanted to do with my life. The more I thought about it, the more I realized that I enjoyed being active in my church and teaching the youth. So, it seemed to me that the most logical path would be to go into the ministry. I marshaled my courage and told my pastor and my dad that's what I felt called to do.

My dad said, "Well, if God is telling you that you that's what you need to do, then that's what you need to do."

So I started making applications to seminaries, and soon after I did, I became physically ill. I prayed and prayed and had the strong sense that God did not want me to go to seminary. This was not His will for my life.

So I stopped and said, "Lord, I don't know what to do. Please show me what you want me to do." I was baffled, stymied, and heartbroken because I simply did not know how long I could go on in the appliance business. I did not find the work satisfying at all. It simply did not feel like what I was meant to be doing with my life.

Then one day, seemingly out of the blue, my dad called me into his office.

He said, "Peter, the big box retailers are coming to this area, and they are going to be selling appliances. I want you to consider going to law school. Your brother's in real estate. We own lots of real estate—that's our future. Being a lawyer would be a tremendous complement to what we do."

I thought, *Law school? I don't even like lawyers.*

Outloud, I said, "Gee, Dad, I don't know. I've never thought about going to law school."

Dad said, "Well, why don't you pray about it?"

"Okay, then. I will."

And I did. I prayed saying, "You know, Lord, I have been thinking that I want to study the Scriptures. I want to learn more about you. I've never even thought about law.

Is this what you want me to do? I mean, I would go if there were such a thing as a Christian law school."

That night I turned on the CBN 700 Club on TV and watched Pat Robertson say, "We now have a Christian law school."

Wow, that was quick, I thought. *Okay, I'll make an application.*

I had an early interview and got in to Regent University School of Law in Virginia Beach. Dad didn't want to let anyone know right away because he wanted to announce to the staff at the right time and in the right way. So I had to keep it quiet, which made it difficult to look for someone to replace me as manager of the retail appliance business.

"Okay, Lord," I said. "What about a manager for Scalzo Appliances? I can't leave my dad in the lurch."

The next day, a competitor's business manager walked through the door.

"Can we talk?" he said.

We hired him.

"Okay, Lord, thanks for that. Now, what about a tenant for my house?"

At that time I was on the pastoral search committee at my church. We hired one, and of course, the new pastor needed a house.

He rented mine.

The following Sunday I was talking with the woman

who ran the nursery at Church, and she asked me if I was going to help with nursery in the coming year.

I pulled her aside.

"Mae," I said. "This is on the QT, but you need to know that I won't be here starting in the fall. I'm going to law school."

"Where?" She asked.

"Virginia Beach."

"That's funny. We own a four bedroom house there, and we're looking for a tenant."

The house was right next to the law school, and so naturally, we rented it and lived there all three years.

The odds of everything falling into place the way they did were just too long for that sequence of events to have been anything other than a message from God that law school was the direction He wanted me to take. And so, we moved to Virginia Beach in 1992 with three young children. Another came while we were there.

Looking back, I have to say it was quite an adventure. Leslie loved it—a southern girl at heart, she was happy to leave the cold winters of Connecticut behind. Our children loved it, too. What child wouldn't want to be so close to the ocean, waves, and sand castles? I, on the other hand, continued to have stress-related stomach problems. I went to a gastroenterologist, who ran some tests, questioned me about what was going on in my life, and came to the conclusion stress was the culprit. Because of a fear of failure, I studied constantly—practically every waking moment I wasn't in class—often with three little children circling my feet.

The doctor gave me a prescription. He made me promise to stop studying at noon on Saturdays and not to pick up another book before Monday mornings. It took about six months, but after that, I was okay, and the surprising thing is, I got as much work done as I had gotten done before.

So, we went to the Beach. We made friends, enjoyed the weather and the Christian community there. And I must say, I was happy that God had directed me to that particular law school. In addition to the normal subjects I would have taken elsewhere, I took some common law courses that drew upon the Scriptures, which helped satisfy that deeply-felt urge.

In three short years, we returned to Connecticut. I set up my law practice, and we had two more children for a total of six when in 2005 my cancer journey began.

I'll explain how that came about in the upcoming chapter.

Chapter Two
Cancer Strikes

After we returned to Connecticut in 1995, things were fine for a while, but as stated earlier, life often gets messy and hard to take. I was working long hours as I was part of a prestigious Danbury law firm and there were many expectations on new associates. Not only were my days filled, but many nights as well with community commitments that the firm required me to attend as well as land use hearings representing clients. Not only did I have the firm's clients to represent, I needed to develop my own client base that would generate enough money to support a family of eight—Leslie, six kids, and me. At the same time, Leslie was home schooling the children, which we felt was important, and that meant I was the sole provider. So I was scrambling to earn enough money to get by in a part of the country with a high cost of living.

Looking back, it's clear to me that our relationship suffered as a result of all that financial pressure. With all that busyness, not much time was available to stay connected as a couple. But that was not all. A devastating issue with our eldest daughter would soon confront us. Early in her teen years, she developed a substance abuse problem that got progressively worse as time went by. We'd thought that by homeschooling and thereby instilling a Christian worldview in our children we would be insulated from such things, but we were wrong. Her mounting addiction and deepening downward spiral became a huge disruption. Nothing we did seemed to help. It was her way of dealing with anxiety, and it went on for years. I will not say anything more about that unfortunate time in our lives, however, because it's behind us now, and of course we love her. Eventually, she conquered her addiction demons. She's now thirty, clean, sober, and a productive adult, living on her own and supporting herself.

While in the midst of trying unsuccessfully to help our daughter, we got more bad news in 2003. My mom and dad called us one day, saying they had something to tell us. When we arrived in their kitchen, Dad spoke.

"Your mom has cancer," he said.

I felt like my heart stopped. My mom meant everything to me.

Dad continued, "The doctors found a couple of nodules on her lungs, and they are going to start chemotherapy."

Mom's treatment began and continued, and it was eventually discovered that she did not have lung cancer. It was ovarian cancer that had spread to her lungs, which meant it had already reached Stage Four.

That diagnosis was extremely difficult for me to accept. As you know, Mom was one of my go-to people. I could talk to her about anything—tell her anything. And cancer—especially Stage Four cancer—was so totally unexpected because there was significant longevity on Mom's side of the family. My mother's mother was already in her nineties and doing great. My mother's grandmother lived to the age of 103.

It also didn't help that I'd always been fearful of debilitating illnesses. I didn't like to go into hospitals—didn't want any part of them, or cancer—especially cancer. I recall that Leslie had an Aunt Suzy, for example, a beautiful Christian woman I was very fond of, who was stricken with the disease. We visited her toward the end of her life, and it was incredibly distressing and depressing to me. I could barely look at her. She was on an I.V. and she was bloated from the medications. It was so, so sad. She passed away at the age of 42, and I was devastated.

As you know, I'd been tagged "the sensitive one," and so I had a habit of stuffing my feelings from an early age. Now I know to look behind the anger or fear to see what's causing it, but I didn't learn that until much later. Back then, I wasn't able to recognize, acknowledge, and express what was going on inside, which meant I didn't deal with problems or grief in a healthy or productive way. And perhaps the worst thing was happening that I could possibly imagine. My dear, cherished mom had cancer and wasn't expected to live. I was beside myself and didn't know what to do. So I called out to the Lord, "Lord, I don't know how to cope with this. Help me, please!"

I felt the Lord say, "Write a letter."

So I sat down and wrote a four-page letter. I told Mom how much she meant to me and what a wonderful mom she was. When I handed her that letter, I felt a huge burden lifted from me. I guess it was what got me to the final stage of grief—acceptance of the inevitable.

When the doctors had determined it was Stage Four, they'd said she'd only live a few months, but she actually held on for two more years. That brings my story to 2005, perhaps the worst year of my life, starting in January when my grandmother, my mother's mother died. Beginning in 2004 and into 2005, I was having health issues. I felt a lot of pressure—I'm not sure the best way to describe it. It was in the area of my scrotum and the bladder area. Plus I had a lot of hematuria—visible blood in the urine. I was also exhausted most of the time—extremely fatigued. One urologist diagnosed it as a prostate issue, and gave me antibiotics. But I didn't get better, and so I went to another urologist and he also diagnosed it as a benign prostate issue.

The illness—whatever I had—didn't make sense to me, or to anyone for that matter, the doctors included. I should have been in good health. I was 43 years old. I exercised every day. I ate well and took vitamin supplements. Leslie was a good cook who always prepared healthy food. My weight was good. But by the spring of 2005, I had been seeing blood in my urine and not feeling well for about a year. So I went back to my family doctor and told him something must be seriously wrong.

I said, "I can't continue to live like this."

He sent me to a lead local urologist, who had my urine tested. There were no cancer cells in it, and so he thought it was probably benign prostatitis. He didn't seem to think there was anything serious going on, but he said, "Well, let's take some x-rays."

After examining them, he scheduled a time for me to have a cystoscopy in his office—a procedure done by inserting a scope into the penis and pushing it into the bladder to examine the bladder on the inside.

As I watched, I could tell the doctor didn't like what he was seeing.

He pulled out the scope and said, "You have nodules in your bladder."

"What does that mean?"

"You have cancer," he said.

He turned and started to walk out of the room.

I grabbed him. "What do you mean, I have cancer?"

"Well, these types of tumors are almost always cancer. I'm going to have to go in, scrape them, and grade them." He said, "I'm going to have to do what's called a TURBT (transurethral resection of bladder tumor)."

Basically, in that procedure, the doctor puts you under and he goes into the bladder and scrapes the tumor out—or in some cases burns it out—in order to diagnose what's going on. He needs to grade and stage it to see how far it has gone into the bladder wall. The bladder is comprised of an interior area, and then a muscle area, and then an outer area. How deep the cancer has penetrated the bladder, and the grade of the cancer, determine the treatment. Most bladder cancers are low grade, non-invasive, so people can just have scrapings or lasering done, and then get it checked every three months. The nodules and tumors frequently come back, but it's not usually life threatening. Overall, bladder cancer has a very high survival rate.

We scheduled the procedure, and the doctor performed it, but while he was working, my bladder got punctured, and so what was supposed to be an outpatient procedure ended up being a two night stay at Danbury Hospital because of the bleeding. A catheter was inserted in me, which allowed healing to occur because that way the urine went straight out instead of filling the bladder.

About a week later, Leslie and I went to the doctor's office to learn about the pathology.

He walked into the room, scratching his head. I have since learned that when your doctor scratches his head, it is not a good sign.

He said, "Are you sure you never smoked or worked around chemicals?"

"No, never."

Bladder cancer usually happens to men in their sixties or seventies who smoked or worked around chemicals. I was 43.

He said, "I don't know how to tell you this, but you have high-grade cancer."

I thought I was going to throw up.

He said, "You look like you're turning green."

I said, "I need to lie down."

I laid down on the table in the examination room. I knew from research I'd done that most bladder cancers are low grade, non-invasive, and that going forward I could expect to have to see the doctor every three months in order to deal with it. At worst, that would be an inconvenience, but this was totally different. Now I was facing something that could actually take my life.

When I opened my eyes and looked at the ceiling, a voice told me to get a second opinion. I knew right away where to do that because I'd heard of Memorial Sloan Kettering Cancer Center down in Manhattan. When I'd heard Sloan advertise, I'd had a sense that I believe was from the Lord, that Sloan was a place of expertise and healing. I felt that if I ever was diagnosed with cancer, I would go there.

As I lay on the table, in the doctor's office he explained the protocol he had in mind that he'd perform right there in Danbury. It was a treatment called BCG, which is an attenuated live bacterium that causes cow tuberculosis. It's a common treatment for non-muscle-invasive bladder cancer, particularly for cancers that have a risk of worsening over time. BCG is believed to work by triggering the body's immune system to destroy any cancer cells that remain in the bladder after TURBT. That was the protocol recommended.

I tried to listen, but I think I was in shock—I might as well have been hit with a two by four. I'd just been told in so many words that my life might be coming to an end and was entering the grief cycle—denial, anger, bargaining, depression, and acceptance.

I was a long way from acceptance.

When I was able to get up and leave the doctor's office, I walked outside, totally shaken, a huge pit in my stomach, and with the overwhelming feeling things were totally out of control. I sat down on the curb and called my mom.

I wept as I told her the news—I had cancer.

"Darn," she said. "I thought this was going to be easy."

"No . . . I feel like I'm too young to die."

"Well," she said. "Let's just take this a step at a time."

I wondered, where is God? Has He abandoned me? I have cancer. Mom has cancer. How could God have let this happen?

Sloan Kettering took me right away. I made an appointment with Dr. Harry Herr there who is a world-renowned bladder cancer specialist. He was the first to do a radical cystectomy and prostatectomy at Memorial Sloan Kettering in 1984. So he had been there for some time. When I first went to visit him, he also did a cystoscopy right in his office, and it was different from what I'd experienced in Danbury because Sloan was a top-notch institution, usually number one or number two in the United States each year according to *U.S. News & World Reports.*

To my dismay, he saw even more cancer. In just two weeks the cancer had grown inside the bladder. The diagnosis was high-grade urothelial carcinoma, potentially a very deadly variety of cancer, one that chemotherapy is not very effective at combating. So the next question was, what stage was it? Dr. Herr said he needed to go in and scrape the bladder in order to determine the staging because it was very important to know what we were dealing with.

As an aside, you probably know that Stage One is basically cancer that's confined to an organ, which means it can be surgically removed. Stage two is cancer that's a little more advanced. For bladder cancer, that would mean it has invaded the muscle wall and is close to coming outside of the bladder. Still, at that stage, it is usually treatable. As the stages increase, survival rates go down. Stage Three bladder cancer has moved beyond the bladder and traveled to a regional area. Stage four is a total metastatic situation where the bladder cancer has traveled usually to the liver, the lungs, or the brain. It's still bladder or urothelial cancer, but it has traveled, usually through the lymph system and deposited itself in other organs.

So Dr. Herr scraped and graded as an outpatient procedure, and a week later, Leslie and I went down to the city to his office to get the pathology results.

We waited in an examination room. Dr. Herr came in and said, "I'm sorry to have to tell you that we've confirmed that you have high grade urothelial cancer. My recommendation is to remove your bladder, and if it's outside of the bladder, you'll probably live about six months because it's going to go to your brain and everywhere else."

Dr. Herr explained what needed to be done. It became clear the surgery was terribly invasive, as you will see, and once again, I couldn't believe this was happening to me. I felt like I was an actor in a horror movie or living out a nightmare when he described what he would do surgically. Anxiety and fear tightened their grip, and again, that huge pit formed and grew in my stomach. All I could do was turn my focus onto my relationship with the Lord and do my best to lean on Him.

We were supposed to go to dinner in the City that night, but I just couldn't because I was so upset. My stomach was churning. I was thinking, "I've got six kids. I've got other responsibilities, too—a law practice to take care of. Dear God, how can this be happening?" I'm not sure what sort of impact all this was having on Leslie, but I'm sure she was hurting, too. She was married to a man in his early forties who shouldn't have had cancer, but did have cancer, and she was going to have to deal with the inevitable consequences of that. We were both in what you might call a survival mode, trying to figure out how to deal with practical issues going forward, and so we didn't talk about the emotional aspects of what was happening. In fact, looking back, I don't think Leslie and I were ever able to connect emotionally with respect to the cancer journey I was about to begin.

In July I had major surgery, which started the transformative part of my journey. I'd never had major surgery before. It took place early in the morning at Memorial Sloan Kettering, and my brother Paul and Leslie were with me.

I recall lying on the gurney, waiting to be wheeled into the operating room and thinking about my situation. For a couple of months up to that point, things had been getting worse with every step I took in this strange, new cancer world. It was clear I had absolutely no control over what was happening, and so—thank the Lord—He gave me a verse to comfort me. It was Galatians 2:20: "I have been crucified with Christ and I no longer live, but Christ lives in me. The life I now live in the body, I live by faith in the Son of God, who loved me and gave himself for me." (NIV) That's when it became clear that going forward I needed to let go, surrender myself to the Lord, trust, and leave everything to Him. My life and my future—if there was to be one on Earth—were totally in His hands.

I kept repeating that verse to myself, and I felt a tremendous sense of peace come over me. I thought of Job, who endured tremendous suffering, and of Paul, who prayed to God three times to have the thorn removed from his side. Even Jesus in the Garden of Gethsemane before the crucifixion, had said, "Father, if you are willing, please take this cup of suffering away from me." (NIV) God didn't cause those problems, and He didn't cause me to have cancer, but He allowed those things to happen because in each case He had a plan—a better idea. Whatever the cause of the cancer—spiritual warfare or sickness due to a broken body in a broken world—I believe this trial filtered through God's hands first.

I know that's hard even for Christians to accept, but just as gold and silver are refined and made pure by intense heat, I believe the truth is God uses the pain and suffering in our lives to transform us—to make us better, more empathic people, and to bring us closer to Him. In James 1:2-4, James, the brother of Jesus tells us, "Consider it pure joy, my brothers and sisters, whenever you face trials of many kinds, because you know that the testing of your faith produces perseverance. Let perseverance finish its work so that you may be mature and complete, not lacking anything." (NIV) I had a choice to make: surrender and trust or be bitter and angry. I was choosing to surrender, that God wanted me to be broken and powerless in every aspect of my life.

Those were my thoughts before and as I was being wheeled into the operating room. I saw all the techs and surgical support people waiting there for my arrival. They moved me onto the operating table, which I saw was in the shape of a cross, and my hands and arms were stretched out like I really was being laid on a cross. It wasn't nails that would pierce me. It was needles and I.V.'s. Right then I felt the Lord speak to me saying, "I'm going to take the physical cancer out of you." And He added, "And I'm also going to remove the spiritual cancer from you."

I had no clue what that second statement meant, and I was thinking, "What? What does that mean?" as the anesthesia took effect and I went under.

Almost ten years went by before I found out what that meant.

The surgery took two surgeons seven hours. They cut a huge incision from the pubic bone up past the belly button, went inside and removed the bladder and pieces of the ureters. Then they created a new bladder reservoir out of small intestine. Also while they were in there, they removed my prostate. They did so because the cancer often will have traveled to that area. Then they closed me up.

When I woke I lifted the sheet that covered me and looked. I had tubes—drainage tubes, and what they called a "suprapubic catheter" tube coming out of the area where the neo-bladder was because they didn't want urine to fill it until it had time to heal. I felt devastated. There I lay. I had this huge incision and tubes coming out of me. I'd been diagnosed with deadly cancer. I had a wife, six kids, and a law practice, and I needed to keep everything going.

I was in the hospital at Sloan Kettering for 17 days. One reason was that my intestines weren't working because the doctors had taken them out and laid them on a table while they cut pieces from them to create the new bladder. Of course, when they finished, they sewed them up and put them back. But my intestines shut down because of that, which was expected, and it meant I had to survive on liquids administered through an I.V. —I lost 40 pounds while I was there. I also had a nasogastric tube (NG tube) with a suction device that removed everything in my stomach. If it hadn't, I'd have constantly been throwing up. Even saliva has no place to go when your intestines are totally shut down—things have to go somewhere. It was one of the most uncomfortable things I've ever had to endure because it was not a small tube. On top of that, I found out I couldn't do pain meds. I'll never be a drug addict because narcotic pain medication nauseates me. So I was in the hospital with a 12-inch incision held together by staples using Extra Strength Tylenol for pain relief.

Something extraordinary happened during that time. God really spoke to me. He said, "I want you to be transparent about this journey." I didn't fully know what that meant at the time. I just knew that I'd had a personal relationship with the Lord for a long time, had been active in Church, and I had gone to a Christian college. As you know, I had studied Business and Bible, and I also had an Associate of Arts degree from Moody Bible Institute in Bible, so I really enjoyed Scripture. But I didn't know how God was going to use all that, particularly because I knew that if the cancer had traveled outside the area worked on, my surgeon had told me I wouldn't live very long. At that point, I didn't have the pathology results. They had removed a whole bunch of lymph nodes, and the results had not come back. In retrospect, however, I can see that I was entering territory that would involve my complete surrender to Him, and that I would soon come along side others on cancer journeys of their own and be able to pray with and for them, and be transparent with them about my journey. In many cases I found this was a comfort to them. As time when by, I began to realize on a deeper and deeper level that difficult and painful situations in our lives can be a real opportunity for growth. In fact, a verse in the Serenity Prayer states, "Accepting hardship as the pathway to peace; Taking, as He did, this sinful world as it is, not as I would have it . . . "

Let me tell you about my new bladder and what having one was like. Before my surgery, I had called up a few men. Sloan had given me their names and numbers. So I called to find out how they were getting along with their neo-bladders. Actually, you don't have to get a neo-bladder inside. I chose that method, but you can also get an ostomy, which is a pouch worn over a stoma (an artificial opening) to collect stool or urine. The urine goes out from the kidneys and the ureters directly into an external bag. That's what guys over 70 usually have done. It's an easier surgery, and not as many complications are likely. You also don't have to learn how to urinate. Problems with having a neo-bladder inside are that you could end up having to catheterize yourself because you are unable to get all the urine out of your pouch, and the sensation to urinate is completely different. It doesn't originate in the same place. In order to get the urine out of my neo-bladder, for example, I have to sit down and really push. And it's a different kind of pushing.

This reminds me of a funny incident that happened during the 17 days I was at Sloan. Two doctors had operated on me, one of whom was a woman, and she came into my room and wanted to see if I could pee. You see, being able to pee was a big deal. In order to do so, you had to work some muscles you weren't used to working to push the urine out of your of the neo-bladder. So she came in with two nurses, and they plugged up the suprapubic tube, which comes out of your neobladder, so the urine couldn't go up that way, and the doctor pulled out the Foley catheter.

"Okay," she said. "Let's try to pee. Why don't you stand up?"

So when I stood up and my gown fell off, but no matter—I was very focused on seeing if I could pee into a plastic urinal. I was holding the plastic urinal and I was pushing like crazy, and out came a little tinkle-tinkle. I looked up at my female doctor and the two female nurses, and they clapped their hands and yelled, "Yippie!"

I was immediately transported back to when I was two years old, standing over a toilet for the first time with my mom shouting, "Yippie!"

I received a message from God at that moment. When He speaks to me, it's in my spirit and in my heart. The message at that moment was perfectly clear. It was, "This is how I want you to be—just like a little child." And the verse immediately came to mind, "Let the little children come to me, and do not hinder them, for the kingdom of heaven belongs to such as these." (Matthew 19:14 NIV) It was that kind of dependence on Him that God wanted from me as well as non-judgmental, child-like qualities.

During that time, and at other times as well, I got a number of what I call "downloads" like that. It seems to happen whenever I have surgeries—and I've had a lot of them over the years—at least fifteen that involved overnight stays by last count. I've lost track but I'm sure I have stayed in hospitals well over a hundred nights. I get a lot of downloads from the Lord at those times. After that first surgery in 2005, and after all the other surgeries as well, I would get them when I was walking around in the hospital. You heal and recover quicker if you can get up and get out of bed. So, right after surgery—that first day—I was walking around. I would go around and say "Hi" to people who were patients on the floor, and many times they would open up to me about what was going on with them, and before long I would find myself praying with them. It was as if God was beginning a ministry for me, even though I wasn't doing anything other than walking around and being myself. For example, I would walk by someone's room, see another cancer patient in there, and say, "Hey, how are you?"

And they might say, "Not so well."

I would say, "Sorry to hear that."

They would open up completely, and I would end up sharing and praying with them, and it wouldn't be just about physical issues, it would be about spiritual and emotional issues, too. As we would say in a cancer support group that I helped start in 2006, "We want to hook our boat up to their boat, and as the storm is raging, we just want to ride it out with them."

And cancer patients weren't the only people I had conversations with like that. It frequently happened with medical staff as well. It certainly was not because I was giving advice or being preachy. I've never been comfortable doing either. It was just me being me—coming along side, honestly sharing my experiences, having empathy and identifying with them, as well as praying for and with them, and giving them encouragement. I was also able to share what was going on in my heart—how God has provided hope for me that things will happen in a certain way—that he has a plan for each of us. That sort of personal testimony would often give them much-needed hope.

After a while it occurred to me that God had equipped me to walk into other people's hearts and lives—others who were on journeys similar to my own, and others who were simply seeking spiritual guidance. It was not because of something I was doing, consciously. It was something He was doing through me.

There were some mornings, however, when I just didn't feel like getting up, and I would just lie there.

My nurse would look in and say, "You haven't done your laps yet today."

I would do my best to ignore her.

Then the custodian, a Jamaican man, would come into the room. I need to tell you about him. It was the same man practically every day—he would clean and mop the room. He never said anything, but he would always hum the same hymn, "Blessed Assurance," and I would feel the presence of the Holy Spirit come over me like a blanket.

"Blessed assurance, Jesus is mine,
O what a foretaste of glory divine,
Heir of salvation, purchase of God,
Born of His Spirit, washed in His blood."

That would stimulate me to get up and I would do my laps. Sometimes, I would be weeping as I did them because the presence of God was so strong—so powerful. At one point, I looked in the bathroom mirror and said to myself, "I can't believe you are a cancer patient. What are you doing here?" But the feeling I had was that the presence of God's spirit was so strong and thick in that place that there was no other place I'd rather be. I recall actually saying that out loud, "There's no other place I'd rather be than right here."

I recall one time when a lot of fluid had built up, and the doctors needed to install a drain. I was on a gurney waiting for the procedure and there was a young woman on a gurney next to me. She was probably in her late teens, she was shaking, and her mother was standing behind her, holding her head. I asked the mom what was going on, and she said that even though she'd had her bowel removed, the cancer was back. So I took the young woman's hand, and I prayed for her. Then we prayed together. I don't know where she was with the Lord, but lots of things like that have happened when I've been in hospitals—praying with people, or talking with them. That has occurred throughout my hospital stays and surgeries.

When I got out of Sloan Kettering, I went back to my house in Connecticut. One day, I was lying on my bed in my bathrobe with all my tubes and everything, basically feeling sorry for myself. I couldn't work. I couldn't drive. I couldn't do anything, and I said to myself, "Well, at least I have a nice car—my Subaru." And so I decided to walk down to see it. We had a big house, and I was in a second floor bedroom. It would be a big deal to make that trip because the garage was pretty far way.

I passed Leslie in the kitchen, doing dishes or something, and she sort of looked over as if to say, "What are you doing?" But I just made my way to the garage to look at my car. I opened the door, and you won't believe what I saw. The whole front side was smashed in, and I thought, "Oh my gosh. I can't even have a car."

I later learned that my daughter, Hilary, had smashed it, and no one wanted to tell me. So there I was with all those tubes, and I just backed up, closed the door, and I sensed the Lord saying to me, "Who owns that car?"

And I said, "What do you mean?"

And He came back with, "Well, you gave me everything in your life. That's what you told me. That's what you tell people—that I own everything in your life."

I'd been thinking the car was mine, and it occurred to me that God had decided He needed to strip me down to zero, like Job, and rebuild me from scratch. So the question was, how was I going to react? Was I going to be bitter? Throw a tantrum? Or was I going to surrender to Him and trust that he had a purpose in all this even though I couldn't see it then? It was a choice I had to make.

And I heard Him say, "If I want to smash my car. I'll let my car get smashed."

So I said, "Okay, I got it," surrendered to Him, and went back upstairs to bed.

At that time, we lived half a mile from my parents' house. Walking is the my main recovery tool, and so every day I would gather my drainage tubes and bags—I had a Foley catheter—pull myself together, and go over to my mom's house. She was at home, hooked up to I.V.s, and in the end-of-life process. So from August, when I got back from the hospital, until she passed a couple months later, I would visit her often. We would just talk. We would talk about life. We would talk about anything and everything. I spent a lot of time with her. It was a period in my life I'll never forget. I was recovering, and she'd had a major surgery, too. She was recovering, but her prognosis was not good. Mine, on the other hand, was good because all the lymph nodes came back clean. The cancer had traveled up one of my ureters a little, but the doctor said he had cut that out. I basically had clean margins, and he felt good about that. Of course, I felt good about that, too, but overall, it was a tough year. My grandmother passed, Mom passed, and then Leslie's dad passed in December.

That was 2005, the beginning of my cancer journey. Next up, a big scare, a 21-day ordeal, and my spiritual surgery.

Chapter Three
Spiritual Surgery

After my 2005 surgery, I had to see Dr. Herr in New York City for frequent check ups, including CT scans and such, and things with my health went along okay for quite some time. However, something significant to do with cancer did occur in 2006. A survey was conducted at my church, and the question was asked, "Have you, or anyone you know, been affected by cancer?" In a church with 2400 members, the result was that 150 people answered, "Yes."

At about the same time, a man in my church named Keith was diagnosed with colorectal cancer at age 46, and so I gave him a call. He wasn't a fully committed Christian or churchgoer at the time, but he became one, and it turned out that my call launched a very close, six-year friendship. We met or talked on the phone just about every day until he passed at age 52. I was with him when it happened—one of my hands under his head and the other around his body.

Not long after we met in 2006, Keith and I launched the Walnut Hill Cancer Support Group that I mentioned briefly in the last chapter, and I have been the ministry leader of it ever since. As you may recall, the premise is: "We want to hook up our boat to yours and ride out the storm with you." The group does everything we can, from sitting with people during chemo, to bringing them meals. We have prayer shawls that people in the church have knitted. We walk with people through the entire process, whether they recover, or go on to be with the Lord. Countless numbers have been in and through the group, and I've given several eulogies. As I write this, I just got back from hospice about an hour ago, where I was visiting one of our people who is going through an end of life process.

Concerning my health, in 2010 I once again began not feeling well. Mainly, I was experiencing chronic fatigue, and my creatinine levels were rising. As you may know, high levels of creatinine in the blood warn of possible malfunction or failure of the kidneys. In addition, my CT scans were showing some sort of a stricture around the juncture of my ureters and the neo-bladder. That's when Dr. Harry Herr sent me to Dr. Michael Grasso, a world leader and specialist in urology and surgery at Lenox Hill Hospital in New York City. By that time, I'd been free of cancer for five years, and I thought cancer was in my rearview mirror.

Dr. Grasso flushed fluid through my ureters a couple of times. Suspicious cells turned up in the second of those flushes, and Dr. Grasso called me into his office to give me the news. He is sort of person who comes straight to the point. I've since come to appreciate his frankness, but at the time, I found it to be intimidating, and so I will have to say I was a little nervous.

"Looks like we're dealing with cancer," he said.

I felt that huge pit expand inside my stomach and was instantly gripped by fear. Cancer had returned! That was the indication. I would again be facing death, and I had to undergo another major operation—this time in 2011 at Lenox Hill.

Dr. Grasso and his surgical team redid my entire urinary system, including the ureters and the part of the neo-bladder where it connected to the ureters. Again my intestines were pulled out and placed on the table, and tissue was cut from them. I spent 21 days in the hospital and had all the same tubes and recovery issues as before, including the nasogastric tube (NG tube) with a suction device that removed everything in my stomach. Once again, I lost 40 pounds.

Happily, however, the pathology following that surgery did not show there had been any cancer. What a relief! What Dr. Grasso found when he opened me up was that my appendix was inflamed—it was almost ready to burst—and it had plastered itself to the area where a ureter and the neo-bladder were connected. That had been the problem, and following a long hospital stay, I recovered.

The next major surgery took place in 2014. That's when I had the "spiritual surgery" the Lord had promised He would perform. As you recall, I'd heard Him say that when I was on the operating table in 2005 and was on the way under from the anesthetic. Following that surgery, I had a strong sense that I did not have control over many things in my life, but that my very existence was in God's hands. I came to realize that I had a significant amount of rubble in my life, and it was hindering my connection with Jesus. However, in 2014, I was about to experience a very significant spiritual event in my life: having poverty of spirit. After all, Jesus says, "Blessed are the poor in spirit, for theirs is the kingdom of heaven" in the Sermon on the Mount (Matthew 5:3 NIV). To me being poor in spirit means coming to a place in life when you have clarity on how broken you are and that you are unable to fix yourself—that you need to turn your life over to a Higher Power. I was feeling broken in my marriage and broken as a man. Leslie and I were not communicating on an emotional level, and I was struggling with my own issues. I was trying to control what was going on in my life, but I couldn't. It was increasingly apparent my efforts were futile. I had the feeling that "I cannot handle this—I'm bankrupt within myself and need God to take my hand and lead the way." I think the point I finally reached is best illustrated in Scripture by the story Jesus tells of the Prodigal Son.

More than likely, you know this parable. A father has two sons, a younger and an older. The younger son asks the father for his inheritance, and the father grants his son's request. However, the younger son is prodigal (i.e., wastefully extravagant) goes off to a foreign land and squanders his fortune on wine and women. Eventually, having lost everything, he has to take a job tending pigs, which of course for Jews like himself are unclean animals. The prodigal son has become so destitute and so hungry, he is more than willing to eat the slop he has to feed to the pigs.

That's when Scripture quotes Jesus as saying, "When he came to his senses, he said, 'How many of my father's hired servants have food to spare, and here I am starving to death! I will set out and go back to my father and say to him: Father, I have sinned against heaven and against you. I am no longer worthy to be called your son; make me like one of your hired servants' (Luke 15:17-19 NIV).

Of course, the father does nothing of the kind. He welcomes his son home with open arms and even throws a huge party to celebrate his return.

To me, coming to the point reached by the prodigal son when he "came to his senses" is what is meant by "poverty of spirit." He realized how terrible a mess he had made of things, and that he needed to turn his life over completely to his father. That's the point I reached going into my spiritual surgery. I was trying too hard to be the one in control, and God showed me the destruction caused by that. In a way, I had a "coming to my senses" time, a point at which He gave me clarity of my sin. I then knew I had to surrender everything to Jesus.

Another way of describing the "coming to my senses" time or poverty of spirit is the concept of brokenness as the Bible depicts it. Because I grew up in the church, I love the story about King David. King David is highly regarded as one of the most famous leaders of ancient Israel and described as a "man after God's own heart." In 2 Samuel 11, the Bible records the scene of David on his rooftop when he spots a married woman, Bathsheba, bathing on another rooftop. He summons her, has relations with her and she conceives a son. To make matters worse, Bathsheba was married to Uriah the Hittite, who was a very loyal soldier in David's army. In David's effort at a cover up, he tried to get Uriah to sleep with his wife Bathsheba so that when the baby came Uriah would think it was his. However Uriah was so loyal to David and the army, he would not leave their sides to be with Bathsheba. Eventually, David had Uriah killed by intentionally putting him in harm's way on the front line of battle with the other men pulling back. Lying, deceit, lust, adultery, murder, and so forth—that's quite a list for the King of Israel. David did come to his senses, however, repented and experiences "poverty of spirit." In his time of brokenness, David records the following about what God desires (Psalm 51:16 - 17- NIV).

You do not delight in sacrifice, or I would bring it; you do not take pleasure in burnt offerings. My sacrifice, O God, is a broken spirit; a broken and contrite heart you, God, will not despise.

I believe God values a broken and contrite spirit because of what it does for those who have one. I don't think it means to be beaten down in judgment and condemnation, but to get clarity of our sins and character defects. In other words, "We come to our senses." For me, being in a place to receive clarity of my brokenness has involved humility— a place where I realize it is not about me. It is about Jesus in me. I am capable of responding to life in very destructive ways, which is why I need a deep connection with Jesus. I need to surrender and to put Him in charge.

Let me take a minute to describe an image that I truly believe was given to me by God of what it's like to put Jesus in charge. I see myself in the back seat of an old family station wagon, one with wood paneling on the sides. I'm a little boy, playing with my toy soldiers or superheroes, and I'm totally content. Jesus is in the driver's seat. His hands are on the wheel, and a smile is on His face. The windows are down, a summer breeze is flowing through the car, and Jesus' hair is ruffled by it. I have no idea how to drive. I have no idea where the car came from. I have no idea were it gets gasoline, or how it operates. I don't know where it's going or where Jesus is taking me. I'm in this place of surrender, and I feel great. I'm living the Serenity Prayer, a little of which I quoted earlier. Here it is in its entirety:

God, grant me the serenity
to accept the things I cannot change,
the courage to change the things I can,
and the wisdom to know the difference.

Living one day at a time,
enjoying one moment at a time;
accepting hardship as a pathway to peace;
taking, as Jesus did,
this sinful world as it is,
not as I would have it;
trusting that You will make all things right
if I surrender to Your will;
so that I may be reasonably happy in this life
and supremely happy with You forever in the next.

So, going into my spiritual surgery in 2014, my broken-ness and pain drove me to a place where I needed to put Jesus in the driver's seat. I'd realized I couldn't handle the journey on my own and had turned it over to Him. Even though that was the case, however, I was spiritually and emotionally guarded. There were sins and there were de-fects in me I wanted and needed to confess to others but there wasn't a safe place for me to do it. As a result, I only let people see the tip of the iceberg—the small part of me above the water line that I was willing to let show.

Another way to put this is that my spirituality was mostly "outward," if that makes sense. I had been active in evangelical churches for 42 years. I would go every Sunday with my big study Bible in hand, my trophy wife and my six seemingly successful children in tow, and I would do much more than simply listen to a sermon. I was a very ac-

tive elder in a church with 2400 members. I not only wor-
shipped along with everyone else, I served on committees,
volunteered my time, led study groups, and much, much
more. In other words, I would do all the outward things—
and even more than all the outward things—that a good
Christian would do. But even so, something on the inside
was continually nagging at me. In retrospect it's clear, the
outside looked good—you could say, even outstanding—
but I had serious problems on the inside. What I didn't know
yet was that I needed to get out of a state of denial, determine my character defects and sins, examine them, and then
I needed to confess them to myself, to God, and to others.

I have found that for me, change comes most often
through pain. What I needed was for Jesus, my Higher
Power, to transform me, and it began because Leslie and I
saw a faith-based, Christian counselor. Part of this therapist's process was for us to take personality tests. The results of my test showed that I was struggling with anxiety
because I was getting my value from pleasing people and
performance. In other words, the underlying, driving motive
of my actions was to receive recognition. When I didn't get
it, I became mired in negative thinking as well as anger and
resentment toward others. It was obvious that from a Biblical standpoint, what I needed to do was to focus on "the log
in my own eye" rather than "the splinter in my brother's

eye" (See Matthew 7:1-5). To come directly to the point, the therapist told me I had a lot of issues.

"You are a very screwed up, very codependent guy," she said.

My transformation began, and continues today, in the context of Celebrate Recovery® [CR], a program started by the author of *A Purpose Driven Life,* Rick Warren's Saddleback Church about 25 years ago. You might describe CR as a Christian twelve step program infused with the Beatitudes, which I knew something about because of my daughter who'd suffered, and eventually had recovered from substance abuse addiction. Even though I was already aware of CR before I saw the counselor, I had avoided taking part in it because I thought it was only for addicts, and I certainly didn't consider myself to be an addict. But having begun working with the counselor, I had taken the first step—no pun intended—and before I knew it, she had me on the path to recovery.

The therapist was located in Texas, and I had a Skype appointment with her once a week for a year. The first thing she and I did was to conduct a thorough Step Four inventory on me. Once that process was underway, I simultaneously began a step study in Connecticut with a small group of men at my church.

Step Four is when you really dig into your past and your personality to see what the underlying causes are of your issues. We began there because I had already covered steps one through three. I'd admitted I was powerless and that my life was unmanageable. I wasn't sure what my issues were at that time, but I knew I was broken. That's Step One. Step Two is to recognize you need a Higher Power, and I already had a relationship with Jesus. Step Three is about turning your life and your will over to the Higher Power, which I had also already done.

Looking back, I didn't know what was wrong, or what the Step Four inventory would reveal, and that is not surprising. Most people don't know what's wrong until they go through the process. Like a lot of people, I had been in denial and was blind to things, and so in order to find out, we looked into my past with what is called, "Spiritual Mapping." I should point out that we also looked for good things. No one's situation or past is all negative or bad. There has to have been some good, and so to keep from becoming mired in abject negativity, it's important to keep as much balance as possible between the good and the bad.

You might say Step Four is the nitty-gritty, close-up-and-personal heart of spiritual surgery. It's like viewing yourself under a microscope, and so we looked at different stages of my life—the formative years from birth to 13, then the period from 14 to 22, and finally, the adult years—and we mapped them. I identified people that had hurt me and people I had hurt. The concept here was not to dwell on the past and blame others but rather to deal with the past, to get clarity on why I had some of the issues I had, and to discover what my part was—my character defect or sin. Then, when the mapping was done, we made a list of character defects, and twenty-one of them bubbled up to the surface.

As an example of mapping an individual, consider my Dad. He was very performance oriented, and so the message I'd received from him was that a person's value equated to his or her work ethic and performance. As you know, my father came from an immigrant family that owned a small business. For them, everything was about work, and a person had high value if he or she was a hard worker. I think it is absolutely positive to instill and communicate the message that being productive and working hard are good attributes. However, as a codependent person, I was looking to others for my value, including my Dad. Therefore, I thought if only I could perform well and achieve titles and accolades in life, I would have value. I worked hard at my job, I achieved a law degree, and I held many positions of authority, and was very involved in my community. I thought this would bring me feelings of worth and value. I also carried this same performance-based value into my relationship with God. I thought, "God will be really pleased with me if I perform really well and achieve titles in the church." I thought the pinnacle of it all would be to lead others and eventually become an elder. I became an elder, and I still wanted more. Finally, when I was at that place of brokenness, I realized that my value and worth are not dependent on performance or perfectionism, but rather, they came from the abiding and unconditional love my Lord had for me. He loved me when I was resting, watching a movie or in a non-performance mode. God does not love me for what I do, he loves me for who I am—He loves me for me. I can honestly say that I had resentment towards my Dad and others, and it was totally on my part and undeserved. I have confessed and worked through that resentment and unforgiveness. I was connecting the dots of the character defects I was experiencing at the time, which had their roots in my past—including my early formative years. I continue this practice today.

I also struggled with feelings of unworthiness, which led me to become a people pleaser whose sense of worth and value was derived from others. Inside, I harbored anger, resentment, bitterness, and underneath it all, a sense of worthlessness. In high school I turned to alcohol and lust—coping mechanisms like that. When I met Leslie, I could not believe that she actually liked me. What did I bring to her of value? I believed people had value if they were good looking, good athletes, really popular in school—that sort of thing. I had an unhealthy view of what value really was. I carried that perception of value into my relationships, including my marriage and even in terms how I felt God viewed me. Again, since I was a little boy, I thought, "If I can only please others and have value in their eyes, I will truly be a person a value." I know now it doesn't make sense that I would derive my value from broken humanity—from the perceptions of others—and when I did not receive what I was looking for from others, I would be resentful and critical. I was camped out in a place of negative thinking. Imagine how wonderful it became for me when I finally realized my value came from God—the unconditional lover who created me.

The bottom line of the Step Four inventory was for me to honestly and humbly face the character defects that were rooted in my past. There were 21 of them, mainly having to do with codependency, such as getting my value and worth from people and performance, as well as perfectionism, resentment, dwelling on past hurts, anger, fear, anxiety, and feelings of worthlessness. For my entire life up until that point in 2014, I had been playing and replaying destructive lies in my head and heart about myself and about others. But, thank the Lord, I was about to experience the healing and freedom in my life that I had always yearned for.

As an "extra" to my Step Four process, I engaged in a process called "Walking in Truth" for each character defect. Today I still use this tool as I go through my exercise of a daily inventory. I make a note to document when I experience a character defect, I write what does God have to say about that defect, and I say a prayer of confession to God and thank Him for a new perspective based on His truths.

For example, I would ask myself, when did I experience anger, or performance based thinking, or fear and anxiety? I would journal that. Then I would go to the Scriptures as the next step to determine what God had to say about it. After that, I would draft my prayers to be read every day during my time with the Lord. For example, I would get angry when I didn't measure up to my standards, and I would get mad with other people when they didn't measure up to my standards. I wanted situations to go the way I wanted them to go, and when they didn't, it would set me off. So I wasn't accepting people for who they were.

After taking time to find out about what God had to say about that, I realized my anger wasn't a righteous or a Godly anger. It was selfish and about me not accepting people and situations the way they were. I came to realize that we all are at different places on our journeys. I'm on my journey. They each are on theirs. Who am I to expect someone else to be at a different place? I needed to focus on my journey and on, "my side of the street," as we say in CR. So my prayer was that God would help me to accept those things I can't change and to accept hardship as a pathway to peace.

I told myself, "Peter, you must accept this. You don't have control over very much in life. The only thing over which you have complete control is how you're going to respond to things. You don't have control over other people, places, or things." Coming to grips with that was a big part of the healing process. God's surgery on me was carving out things like the anger in me. I call it, "Removing the rubble between me and the Lord," and it means letting people see the iceberg underneath the water.

When I began my journey into my Step Four inventory with my therapist, my good friend Johnny D, who started CR in our church, encouraged me to join a Step Study with other men. Then I began to attend CR large group meetings where there are lessons, worship and testimonies. The first CR testimony I heard was from Katharine, one of the CR leaders. It was so transparent, vulnerable and honest about her character defects and family issues that I said to myself, "I will never get up and reveal all of my stuff to others like this." About one year later, after my Step Study and working with my therapist, I was up front in the large group meeting delivering my testimony: being open, honest and transparent. It was terrifying and yet exhilarating. I felt loved by the group. One year after becoming a small group leader in CR, I became the Ministry Leader. It has been a life-changing journey, and I thank God for it.

According to the Celebrate Recovery® website, the program is now available in around 35,000 churches around the world. I have been the CR Ministry Leader in our church now for over two years. As indicated above, the CR process involves working through the twelve steps, but the Beatitudes are infused into the CR program as well, and Jesus is the Higher Power. There are eight principles we work through, and something that's very important, it all takes place in the context of complete anonymity and confidentiality—we are very strict about that. No one is there to "fix" you, there can be no cross talk, and only "I" and "me" statements are allowed. There also are no graphic descriptions allowed, and everything that's said, and the identities of who was at the meeting, must stay in the room. This creates a safe place for everyone.

I have to admit I didn't feel safe at church until after we started the Celebrate Recovery® program. When other people began confessing their problems, I no longer felt defensive because they were telling me about their issues and I was telling them about mine. The best way to describe it is that I was working on the log in my own eye and didn't even see the speck in my brother's (see Matthew 7:3-5), and so it became incredibly freeing and healing. As we say in CR, "to reveal is to heal, and you're only as sick as your secrets." It enabled me to confess things and discuss things and drill down into why I did this or that. Because of the meetings and my therapy, I became aware of myself and saw the man in the mirror for the first time. There were things I saw I didn't like, but I was willing to bring them out into the open. As a result, God really healed me and brought me a lot of victory in those areas. I still struggle, but He has done a great work in me, and so I consider the entire CR process to have been the spiritual surgery God had promised.

To expand a little more on the Celebrate Recovery® program itself, I would say only about one-fourth to one-fifth of the individuals in our meetings actually struggle with drugs and alcohol. There are people that suffer from porn and sex addiction, food and substance abuse, codependency, anger, depression, anxiety, physical, sexual and emotional abuse from the past. People use CR to work through practically every issue you can imagine. We like to call it "Celebrate Transformation" due to the growth we experience both spiritually and emotionally, for any habit, hurt or hang-up. Because we create a safe place, we are encouraged to be honest about our sins and character defects with ourselves, with God and with others. We are encouraged to walk in God's forgiveness and unconditional love with each other—not in shame and condemnation. In James 5:16, we are encouraged to confess our sins to one another and be healed. I have witnessed healing and freedom in my life and in so many other lives of the participants.

As I mentioned, "Step Studies," where we work through the 12 steps, are held on a different night of the week than the large group meetings. Men work with men and women with woman. I've assisted many others with this—typically I'm the sponsor of three or four guys at any one time. It's a ten-month program with four workbooks. The first three steps are about "peace with God". The second three are "peace with ourselves," and the next three are "peace with others." We conduct the Step Four Inventory in the peace-with-ourselves part, and then we move to, "What does God have to say moving forward," which is seeing what the Scriptures have to say about our issues.

Part of recovery process when you are ready, is about making amends with people you have hurt, and people who have hurt you, which, by the way, is it's not about confronting someone. It's about making amends for your own stuff—the log in your own eye. When you make amends you usually do it in person or by a letter. You say something like, "I'm in a recovery program, and I want to just ask for your forgiveness because I've been angry and unforgiving," or whatever the issue is that you struggle with. The other person might not forgive you, but that's not the point. The goal is to release any un-forgiveness or bitterness or resentment to do with that person, which you might have been holding onto. For example, some of my character defects stem from dwelling on past hurts and being resentful, and so a key part of my healing process was to go to people and to say that I'm sorry so that I could put the hurts and resentment behind me and move forward. I've done it with most of my family—mostly verbally, but also in letters. There actually are still a few more people on my list, but that's okay because it's a process—you never actually arrive at the finish line.

When we introduce ourselves in CR, we say, "I am a grateful believer in Jesus Christ and I struggle with . . ." In other words, our identity isn't with the struggle. Our identity is with Christ, but we acknowledge and recognize that we struggle in certain areas. Usually the common thread is pain. That's typically why people come through the doors to CR—they're in pain. Something in their lives has brought them to a place where they feel powerless. Step One is definitely a key step—that they feel powerless and that their life is unmanageable in certain areas. I believe that when Jesus said, "Blessed are the poor spirit for theirs is the kingdom of heaven" in the Sermon on the Mount, He was actually identifying the gateway to spiritual and emotional growth. Success in healing for me first hinged on coming to the point when I realized that I cannot make the journey by relying on my own strength. For me it was, "I can't, but Jesus can."

Chapter Four
My Dark Night of the Soul

In 2015, right before the Fourth of July, I knew something was wrong because no food or drink was passing through my system. I began to feel nauseated that day and left work early. When I got home, I started throwing up. Leslie was away on a trip to Bali where she was spending time with our daughter, Pearl, who was completing a gap year between high school and college. My two sons were home, but unfortunately, they were in another part of the house with their phones turned off. I was in such a bad state, I was unable to make it to their rooms to get help, and so I spent a long night throwing up.

The next morning, they saw a text I sent, took me to the emergency room at Danbury hospital, and I was hospitalized with a bowel obstruction. An NG tube was installed to suck out the contents of my stomach, and I was there seven days until my digestive system finally quieted down and food began to pass through.

Fortunately, I was back on my feet and well enough to travel after I left the hospital because I had a big vacation trip planned. I was to meet Leslie and Pearl in San Sebastian, Spain. They were to fly there from Bali, but that never happened. Mount Raung in East Java erupted, spewing countless tons of ash into the air and grounding all flights from Ngurah Rai International Airport. I spent seven days in Spain pretty much alone as a result. A friend from Connecticut lived in San Sebastian but wasn't there at the time. He'd provided me with introductions to some of his friends, but they worked during the day, and so I saw them only in the evenings and at night. Rather than a downer and a waste of seven days, however, this turned out to be the answer to a prayer. You see, I had been praying for some "Mary time" with Jesus because my life in the months and years leading up to that trip had been in turmoil because of work, doctors' visits, clinical tests, and the normal messiness of life.

You may be wondering, what is "Mary time"? It is time spent relaxing at the feet of Jesus, and listening. You are probably familiar with the story recounted in Luke 10:38-42 when Jesus was at the home of Martha and her sister, Mary. Here's the New International Version (NIV) translation:

> As Jesus and his disciples were on their way, he came to a village where a woman named Martha opened her home to him. She had a sister called Mary, who sat at the Lord's feet listening to what he said. But Martha was distracted by all the preparations that had to be made. She came to him and asked, "Lord, don't you care that my sister has left me to do the work by myself? Tell her to help me!"
>
> "Martha, Martha," the Lord answered, "you are worried and upset about many things, but few

*things are needed—or indeed only one. Mary has
chosen what is better, and it will not be taken away
from her."*

I believe Jesus is saying that Martha's worries and distractions are preventing her from being truly present with Jesus. I could relate to Martha, and yet I felt an inner longing to have more intimacy with Jesus. In that culture, Martha was doing what was expected of her as well as Mary. However, Mary knew something very special was happening in their home. Mary needed to spend quality time with Jesus. I could relate to Mary's need. I had been asking Jesus for more time with Him.

That week spent with Jesus each day was a special gift He gave me, a true blessing as I see it. I needed that Mary Time listening to Him and recharging my batteries. Mary Time for me is time spent in meditation, time spent clearing my mind, sitting in silence with Jesus. It's about being completely intimate and honest with Him and appreciating his unconditional love and acceptance. It's also time spent in gratitude, thanking Him, and recognizing who He is. Whether it was in my room, or on long walks I would take on the beach, He would be right there with me, and I would tell Him everything that was going on in my life, the desires of my heart, my concerns, my hurts, hang-ups, and where I was falling short. There can be no doubt about it, Mary Time is wonderful time. I could feel His forgiveness and Him wrapping his arms around me. I felt absolutely connected to Him during that week in Spain. Little did I know what would soon be coming my way.

When I returned home, my creatinine levels had begun rising again, indicating a problem with my kidneys. I also wasn't feeling well and had a fever. A problem was that my kidneys were filling up with urine because they had been compromised from the neobladder surgery. When a bladder is removed, the valves that normally stop urine from traveling back up to the kidneys also are taken out.

To relieve the pressure and also to take some biopsies, Dr. Grasso performed an operation on August 31, 2015. I spent three days and nights in the ICU. In addition to the biopsies, he flushed out the ureters, and he installed a tube called a nephrostomy, which drains urine directly from the kidneys into a collecting bag outside the body. That way, the urine bypasses the uterers and the bladder completely. Thankfully, the pathology that came back did not show cancer.

I had another biopsy on September 28, however, that did show cancer, and once again I was gripped by fear. I knew from my research that metastatic bladder cancer had about a five percent survival rate, but Dr. Grasso could not give me a prognosis. He said he wouldn't be able to until he got in there and looked. The bottom line was that I had to have another operation, but before Dr. Grasso would perform it, he wanted to see the results of a PET scan and an MRI. If they showed cancer was outside of the area, he said he wasn't going to operate. If the cancer had metastasized, there would be no point.

Here we go again, I thought, when a major hurdle appeared in the way. My insurance company would not pay for the PET scan and MRI, maintaining it was "not medically necessary." I have learned along the way during my journey that such actions by insurance companies are typical. The PET scan and MRI together would cost about $10,000 and insurance companies are in business to make money. They want policyholders to have to bring an appeal—it's a stalling tactic. Fortunately, a close friend of mine and State rep at the time, David Scribner, went to bat for me as he had already done several times. David represented the 107th District in the Connecticut Legislature. First, he called the president of Danbury Hospital, who agreed the hospital would go ahead with the tests, and worry later about the cost. Then David did battle with the insurance company and won.

The MRI and PET scan came back not showing anything to prevent the operation, and I was cleared for surgery, which took place on November 2, 2015. It had been snowing, and so Leslie and I went down the night before. We got up early the next morning and walked over to Lenox Hill. Dr. Grasso on the other hand was late because there was a problem with the train due to the weather. But he eventually arrived, and I was wheeled into the operating room where a talented and experienced team of three urological surgeons headed by Dr. Grasso worked on me for ten hours. One reason it took so long was that there was a lot of scar tissue to cut through, and once inside, they saw that the situation was much worse than they'd imagined.

It was late at night when Dr. Grasso finally came out to inform my family. My brother Paul told me he said, "Okay, no one talk, so I can tell you what happened." He said that Dr. Grasso reminded him of an NFL quarterback on Superbowl Sunday being interviewed right after the game, a quarterback who'd tried to cover 80 yards in less than a minute and had thrown a hail-Mary pass on the last play of the game. The message was, he and the other surgeons had found a number of complex tumors. One was plastered to my aorta and there were others in and out of my ureters. Tumors seemed to be all over the place.

Even later that night, Dr. Grasso came into my room in the ICU, sat down next to me and said that what they had found was much worse than they'd anticipated. He went on to say that at one point during the surgery, the three surgeons looked up and said to each other, "What do we do next?" That reminded me of when I first woke up in the ICU after the surgery and saw what looked like plumbing drawings next to my head. Dr. Grasso had made them when he was trying to figure out what to do.

Besides removing all the tumors they could see, he had to redo my whole system, including the ureters and sections of the neobladder. As evidence of how bad it was, Dr. Grasso wrote in a letter, a copy of which I have in my possession, saying that in his "vast experience in reconstructive surgeries," it was "one of the most complex [surgeries ever] performed in urology." Not long ago, he also told me he'd given a talk in Amsterdam and in Berlin to hundreds of medical professionals about that operation and my medical history.

What really brought me down, however, was that the situation was a bad as it was. Dr. Grasso told me I was going to need powerful chemotherapy. He said that he and the other surgeons had gotten all the tumors, but he was almost certain that cancer cells remained inside me.

After telling me that, he got up and left, and I have to say, I felt absolutely hopeless. As I lay there, I lifted the sheet and looked at another long vertical incision with tubes coming out from everywhere, and I said to myself, "I can't do this anymore. I can't do it spiritually, emotionally, and physically." I was spent, exhausted, and the night that followed was the absolute worst of my life. It was a night of pain, nagging fear, anger, and deep, abiding sadness. It was my, "Dark night of the soul," a phrase that comes from a poem written by the 16th-century Spanish mystic and poet St. John of the Cross—in Spanish, *La noche oscura del alma*. The poem narrates the journey of the soul to mystical union with God.

Leslie and my son Paul were at my bedside the next morning when I woke up, and I broke down in despair and wept. That is something they had never seen before because, as you know, up until that time it had been my practice to stuff my feelings and not show my emotions.

My son Paul stayed with me for the next week reading scripture and playing hymns. I knew that my family, friends, and church leadership were praying for me, but I felt numb emotionally and spiritually. The thing is, they had been praying I would be healed, that my health would be fully restored and everything would be fine, but that had not happened—far from it.

I got a text from a Church friend named Johnny D that said, "Hey, how are you doing?"

I texted back, "It's dark and getting darker."

He texted, "I'll see you in the morning."

Johnny D said that after he got that text from me he prayed about what to do. He got down on his knees and said, "Lord I have no clue. I am clueless what to tell this man. What can I do?"

The message that came back to Johnny D was clear. The Lord said, "He needs to write. He needs to express what he's feeling. Bring him a journal."

Johnny D showed up in my room at Lenox Hill the next morning and slapped a brand new journal on my chest.

I thought, "What are you doing here, and what is this?"

He didn't stay long, and I put the journal aside.

After about four days I picked it up.

The first journal entries I made were raw and depressing, but I felt I had to be honest about how I felt. An important thing I'd learned from my spiritual surgery, which had just taken place, was not to stuff my feelings.

Here's some of what I wrote:

11/2/15: Post surgery [resulted in] one of the worst feelings of my life: dark, empty, death, separation from my loved ones, pain, residue from anesthesia and drugs. The first night was hellish/horrible. God help me! God, where are you?!

Dr. Grasso—cancer was worse than what we thought: more work was required. Not sure if we got it all. You will need high-powered chemo!

No, I don't want it . . . Yet, your will, O'God.

11/3/15: [My son] Paul and Leslie came to see me. I wept. I can't do this—I'm done. . . . I don't know if I can do this.

I told Jesus, "I can't do this anymore. Take me now." I am so tired of cancer, doctors, and hospitals; 14 surgeries, so many nights.

11/11/15: Tonight—9 days later—I still have: PICC line, G-tube, Foley, nephrostomy tube, closed bowels. Lord, I know that death = peace and union with you. But it also means separation from my family. I need to trust you. This is so hard. Impossible for me to do. I feel so weak. Help me!

The entries above are from my dark nights of despair—the place where I found myself camped, a place of deep and abiding fear, anger and sadness. The turning point came for me when I felt the presence of the Holy Spirit and God spoke these words to my heart, "Okay, Peter, I wired you with emotions and right now those feelings of fear, anger and sadness are driving your bus. But I have a better way for you, a path back to wholeness, healing and restoration." Over the time I was in the hospital and even for a few days following that, He gave me a total of 23 truths that I wrote down in my journal, which helped turn my outlook around. My situation did not change, but one by one those truths lifted my spirits out of the dark pit I'd been in. It happened because I made a decision to focus on those truths rather than dwell on what had been sucking the life out of me. I called it "walking in truth." Even though I didn't feel like it, my spirit and attitude changed as I focused on the life-giving truths God was blessing me with. As I processed these truths, I was overwhelmed with God's presence, and His love for me.

It seems to me that sometimes, particularly when we are in the grip of despair, we don't feel God's presence. Nevertheless, as Christians, we know He is always there, and so we have a decision to make when we reach that point. We must decide if we are going to wallow in grief and turn our backs on God, or are we going to look to Him for guidance, comfort, and grace. That was the point I'd reached, and frankly, at the time I felt I'd failed. I thought, "I'm supposed to be trusting in God and yet here I am down deep in this pit of despair and hopelessness. Obviously, I'm not putting my trust in Him." Yet, at the time, I just couldn't bring myself to do so.

Even though that was the case, however, I never felt that God was disappointed in me. I've come to the conclusion He does not want us to put on a happy face and pretend everything is going along just fine when it isn't. I don't believe He gets upset with us because we are honest about our circumstances. As I wept and told Jesus that I was sorry that I camped out in a negative place of despair that I had created, I felt Him wrap His arms around me in unconditional love and forgiveness. It was a beautiful moment of pure love and acceptance. I will never forget it. I was His son and He understood. In fact, I believe He wept with me in that moment. It was amazing. I knew that he loved and embraced me no matter what, just as He had embraced David, Job, and yes, even Jesus. Things got so bad for Job, for example, that he wished he had never been born. And in Psalm 22:1 (NIV), David is quoted as saying, "My God, my God, why have you forsaken me?" Moreover, as everyone knows,

Jesus repeated that same verse when He was on the Cross—and in agony.

Even though I felt defeated, I believed that my situation had first filtered through God's hands, and that He was still in charge of my life. Colossians 1:13 refers to a transfer taking place—from the kingdom of darkness to the Kingdom of Jesus. This is what happens when we put our trust in Jesus. I also knew from Scripture that I was considered a citizen and an adopted son in that Kingdom, and according to 1 Corinthians 6, that my body is a temple, housing the Holy Spirit—that I am not my own and have been bought with a high price. As I lay in bed, I was comforted by the fact that this cancer diagnosis did not take God by surprise—it had been filtered through His hands first. This reminded me of God's plan and purpose in my life. It still does. I have been told six times in 15 years that I have cancer. My doctor at Memorial Sloan Kettering has twice told Dr. Grasso to send me home and to contact hospice. It happened both after this event in 2015, and later, in 2017. The Book of Job relates an event in heaven when God gave Satan permission to bring destruction and harm to Job. God also gave the enemy permission to inflict the Apostle Paul with a thorn in the flesh. In both cases, God didn't cause the actual harm but, He did allow it to happen.

So there I was like David and Job wallowing in self-pity, but even in the midst of my failure, He was able to do an amazing thing in my life. He was able to lift me up with the truths He gave. Each time I received what I came to think of as one of His downloads, I would weep. Each time one came, I would feel the presence of the Holy Spirit increase. I felt God—as the Father He is—was bringing me gifts and embracing me with love and acceptance. He was in the process of restoring our relationship. The truths were reminders of Him and proof of His unconditional love.

That He loves me, and that nothing can separate me from His love is huge. When the Holy Spirit gave me that truth, I knew that God had been with me in surgery, and in intensive care, and that that He was with me then, in recovery. It came to me in these powerful words below written by the Apostle Paul in Romans 8:38-39. Here is the New Living Translation [NLT]:

And I am convinced that nothing can ever separate us from God's love. Neither death nor life, neither angels nor demons, neither our fears for today nor our worries about tomorrow—not even the powers of hell can separate us from God's love. No power in the sky above or in the earth below—indeed, nothing in all creation will ever be able to separate us from the love of God that is revealed in Christ Jesus our Lord.

Another powerful verse is Romans 8:28 [NIV]:

And we know that in all things God works for the good of those who love him, who have been called according to his purpose.

The verse above assures us that even though we may not see anything good coming from whatever circumstance we are dealing with, in the end things are going to work out, whether it is in this world or the next.

And of course, Psalm 23 is one of my favorite Scripture passages. Here is the New International Version (NIV) translation:

The Lord is my shepherd, I lack nothing. He makes me lie down in green pastures, he leads me beside quiet waters, he refreshes my soul. He guides me along the right paths for his name's sake. Even though I walk through the darkest valley, I will fear no evil, for you are with me; your rod and your staff, they comfort me. You prepare a table before me in the presence of my enemies. You anoint my head with oil; my cup overflows. Surely your goodness and love will follow me all the days of my life, and I will dwell in the house of the Lord forever.

He also said to me, "Peter, when you're weak, then I am strong in you." He also gave me an assurance of eternity with Him, a certainty that when I pass from this earthly tent, I will be with Him forever. And there was this passage from John 13:7 (NIV):

Jesus replied, "You do not realize now what I am doing, but later you will understand."

This verse refers to the Apostle Peter's misunderstanding about Jesus washing his feet. Often Jesus is at work, and we do not see His plan. God's ways at times are mysterious.

I realized the fleeting nature of life on this earth—that my body was actually very fragile. I looked down at my body lying in that hospital bed, with all the tubes and incision. It looked so fleeting and powerless. I heard God whisper in my heart and my spirit that what was important was my surrender and trust in Him—my physical body was temporary, but my spiritual body was eternal. I loved that moment of clarity! Even in the devastation of disease and cancer, the Lord could use it all to draw me closer to Him and deepen my relationship with Him. My body was failing. Yet there was so much hope. He was my God and I was his son. God gave me such a beautiful assurance of what was ultimately important, and that He had an eternal home for me—with Him. I knew where He wanted my perspective and outlook to be, as the passage below from 2 Corinthians 4:16-18 indicates:

Therefore we do not lose heart. Though outwardly we are wasting away, yet inwardly we are being renewed day by day. For our light and momentary troubles are achieving for us an eternal glory that far outweighs them all. So we fix our eyes not on what is seen, but on what is unseen, since what is seen is temporary, but what is unseen is eternal.

Another passage of Scripture, which I have briefly alluded to a couple of times, has been a powerful help to me in my cancer journey. It is Luke 8:22-25, when a storm engulfs the boat Jesus and the disciples were on while Jesus slept. Here's the NIV translation:

One day Jesus said to his disciples, "Let us go over to the other side of the lake." So they got into a boat and set out. As they sailed, he fell asleep. A squall came down on the lake, so that the boat was being swamped, and they were in great danger.

The disciples went and woke him, saying, "Master, Master, we're going to drown!"

He got up and rebuked the wind and the raging waters; the storm subsided, and all was calm. "Where is your faith?" he asked his disciples.

In fear and amazement they asked one another,
"Who is this? He commands even the winds and the
water, and they obey him."

I can totally relate to the men in the boat. They are doing everything within their own power to deal with the situation as they become more and more anxious and increasingly think they are going to perish, and yet for them, Jesus is right there with them just as He is in my life. I imagine them bailing water, rowing faster and strategizing how to get through the perilous storm. I think of those times that I have taken matters into my own hands during my cancer journey. The thing I love about this story is that Jesus has the power to calm my storm as well if I will only wake Him up, and surrender to and trust Him. When I do, he promises that he will travel with me, partner with me in it, and when I look at Him, and focus on Him rather than the storm created by my circumstances, I know that I'm going to be okay. I know that Jesus will deliver peace and joy to me in spite of the storm. During those times I can sense Jesus wrapping his arms around me, and I can feel His tangible presence. When that happens I know that God is affirming me as His son. The comfort this gives me is something I want so much to share with others.

This reminds me of something that happened about a year and a half ago. A man I knew to be very intense called and said he wanted to meet with me. I wasn't sure I wanted to, but after praying about it, I said okay.

When we met, he said, "I pray for people, and I quote healing Scripture, and they don't get healed. I want you to tell me why."

I said, "Why don't you ask a theologian or your pastor?"

"No, I want to talk with you because you're in the thick of it."

I prayed silently, *Lord, how do I answer this?* And God gave me the answer.

I said, "For me, I ask Abba Daddy for healing because that's what I would like to have happen, and God either says, 'Yes,' or He says, 'I have a better idea.' I think God often wants to use the trials in our lives to transform us, and in my situation, that has often been the case." I went on to quote and talk about the passage about Paul, who prayed to God three times to have the thorn removed from his side because He said, "My grace is sufficient for you, for my power is made perfect in weakness." (2 Corinthians 12:9, NIV) I can definitely relate to being weak and broken and having to depend on God even for life itself.

I do believe Jesus is our healer, and I can honestly say there have been times that I have been miraculously healed, even when the doctors didn't think it was possible. But it's also my belief that God often allows pain and suffering in our lives as an invitation to transformation. I know for myself that when life is comfortable, I am unlikely to take the essential steps for a deeper walk with Jesus, such as having less of me and more of Him in my life. I believe God did not cause my cancer, nor did He cause the pain and suffering that has come from it, but He did allow it, and he used it to draw me closer to Him, and to transform me.

In Chapter Six we will look closely at what today would be called a "near death experience" Paul had, during which he ascended to heaven and received marvelous revelations. You might say he got an up close and personal look at the glory that will come after death. As a result, however, Paul said that God gave him a thorn in his flesh, which he called "a messenger of Satan," so that he (Paul) would not boast about having been given such a big revelation. Here is what Paul had to say about this in 2 Corinthians 12:6-10 (NIV):

Even if I should choose to boast, I would not be a fool, because I would be speaking the truth. But I refrain, so no one will think more of me than is warranted by what I do or say, or because of these surpassingly great revelations. Therefore, in order to keep me from becoming conceited, I was given a thorn in my flesh, a messenger of Satan, to torment me. Three times I pleaded with the Lord to take it away from me. But he said to me, "My grace is sufficient for you, for my power is made perfect in weakness." Therefore I will boast all the more gladly about my weaknesses, so that Christ's power may rest on me. That is why, for Christ's sake, I delight in weaknesses, in insults, in hardships, in persecutions, in difficulties. For when I am weak, then I am strong.

That, my friends, is the big takeaway from my journey. It's about surrendering and trusting Him, and it's about realizing that I can't, but that Jesus can. More will be written about this in the final chapter, but for now I will say that is the heart of what I have learned. My wish is to encourage others on difficult journeys with the same understanding, hope and comfort I've been given. I want to give testimony to Him because I wouldn't be telling the truth if I didn't say that every day Jesus Christ has given me a tremendous amount of peace, and even joy, in the midst of the tremendous turmoil I've experienced over the last 15 years. On May 1, 2016, I spoke at the Annual Greater Danbury Prayer Breakfast explaining the understanding I know have that, "I can't but He can."

That talk and how it came to be is an interesting story I will briefly relate. I was in an elder meeting at my church when the chairman looked at me and said, "I think you're supposed to be the next speaker at the prayer breakfast." I looked behind me to see who he was talking to. I was pretty sure it wasn't me because there was always a well-known, top-drawer speaker at the event. Besides that, it was not something I wanted to do. When I was young, I had a stuttering issue, and so public speaking was something I avoided if at all possible, particularly something like the Prayer Breakfast. That event is a really big deal people look forward to. You'd expect someone like Franklin Graham or Luis Palau to speak there. It draws a crowd of from 500 to 600 attendees. But I had told the Lord that I would never say "No" when I feel it's something He wants me to do, and so I agreed to be the speaker.

Preparing that talk and giving it was a surreal experience. The morning of the event came, and I was sitting there as a hymn was being sung when I looked down at the program and saw that Peter Scalzo was the speaker. It suddenly hit home that I was the one speaking that day, and all I wanted to do was run to the bathroom and throw up. I got the sweats, was queasy, and silently said, "Please help me, Lord." Shaky though I was, I did manage to make to the podium, and I began reading my speech and was able to continue my talk to the end.

It's amazing how God works. Apparently, the speech was a hit with a number of people. For example, someone told me recently that he had been at the breakfast, heard the talk, and when he left and was driving away that day, he had to pull onto the side of the road and stop the car because he had begun weeping uncontrollably because of that speech. Let me say that he did not have that reaction because of me. I was only the vehicle. It was caused by God working through me.

If you'd like to see and hear that talk, it's on YouTube. Just put the following into the YouTube search feature: "Greater Danbury Prayer Breakfast - Peter Scalzo"

Let me finish this chapter by filling in a few details about the 2015 surgery. I was in the ICU for three or four days following it, and was unable to talk or interact. My son, Paul, stayed with me 24/7 at that time, read me Scriptures and played hymns for me. He and my daughter Chelsea took turns after that, and I was never alone. In all, I was in the hospital for a total of 19 days and could have "nothing by mouth." But I have to say, Dr. Grasso did a couple of things this time that helped. He installed a PICC line to deliver TPN to me, so that I didn't loose 40 pounds again, and he placed a gastric tube through my stomach wall so that I only had to have an NG tube once in a while. PICC, by the way, stands for "peripherally inserted central catheter." It is put into a large vein in the arm and ends in a large vein near the heart and is used to give IV medications. TPN stands for Total Parenteral Nutrition, and it supplies all daily nutritional requirements.

Even though Dr. Grasso and his colleagues removed all the cancer they could see, as you know, he did not think that he and the other surgeons had gotten it all, and so he wanted me to have chemo as soon as I was able. I went to Yale, Sloan, and Phelps and met with oncologists, and each one of them said, "No," because of my poorly functioning kidneys. The tumors that had blocked the urine flow had damaged my kidneys, and now I had Chronic Kidney Disease. The cancer did not have a tumor marker test to show evidence of cellular cancer activity. Since there was no outward evidence of the cancer on the scans, my oncologists were unwilling to administer chemo since it would destroy what little kidney function I had left.

Sometime after the Prayer Breakfast in May of 2016 I had a PET scan that lit up a couple of lymph nodes. As a result, I had a biopsy that required a seven-inch incision, three-hours of surgery, and a night in the ICU. Surprisingly, the pathology came back negative for cancer, and so I had been cancer free for more than six months.

Unfortunately, however, that did not remain the case, as you will see.

Peter

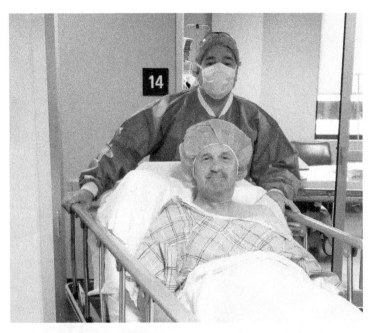

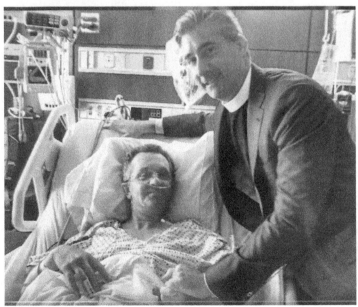

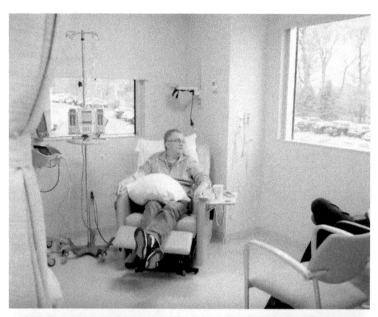

Peter sharing his journey

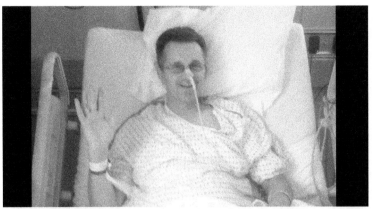

Chapter Five
Gratitude and Hope

Looking back at my "Dark Night of the Soul," there are a few more things that helped pull me out of it that I'd like to tell you about. One comes from the Apostle Paul in 1 Thessalonians 5:18 (NIV), "Give thanks in all circumstances; for this is God's will for you in Christ Jesus." At the time I received this and other truths, I was unable to function on my own. Water and nutrition were being fed to me via an I.V., and I knew that getting up and walking was essential for me to recover because it got my bowels moving and things going. But frankly, I didn't feel I had it in me. I was vacillating between hopelessness and despair, wondering what God could really do in this situation. The medical outlook appeared to be so very bleak. It was like I was paralyzed—in a state of deep depression. It was in that context that I heard God speak to me, asking, "Are you going to be thankful?"

My reaction was, "That's crazy. How can I possibly be thankful in this situation?" It made no sense at all, and yet God brought the verse above to me, reminding me that He actually desires us to give thanks in *all* circumstances, even when we are having a very difficult and messy time, which in my case was an understatement.

Looking back, the amazing thing is, the Scriptures came alive for me, perhaps because of the pain and suffering. They became essential—the lifeline I grabbed onto, and held onto, in order to survive and eventually to thrive. They were precisely the tools I needed when I needed them. Another passage from Paul about gratitude can be found in Philippians 4:6-7 (NIV), "Do not be anxious about anything, but in every situation, by prayer and petition, with thanksgiving, present your requests to God. And the peace of God, which transcends all understanding, will guard your hearts and your minds in Christ Jesus."

In other words, be honest with God, and I was. I told Him everything—that I was struggling with hopelessness and anxiety, and that I was wrestling with fear and anger. I was totally honest, and it helped. But the game-changer came when I told the Lord I was thankful for what He had done in my life. At that point, a switch went off. I believe it was because I saw where God had showed up all through my life.

It's true. When we are honest with God, and make our requests with thankfulness in our hearts and minds, Paul promises peace that transcends all understanding. There's something unique and very special about that. It was clear that I should not be thankful that I had cancer—a source of real harm to me. But I ought to be thankful that Jesus was partnering with me throughout the struggle—I should be thankful for what He was doing in and through the cancer journey. And he had done a lot up to that point.

It also came to me that I should make a list of things in my life I was grateful for—items, people, and events in my life. So I started a gratitude journal, and I made a list of more than 20 things. As I listed items, I soon realized I had a lot to be thankful for—for how much God had done in my life—that He had been a part of my entire life journey and had blessed me in so many ways—for example, growing up in the family that I did and in the part of the world where I was born. And of course, there were the friends I'd made, the great schools I'd attended, how my relationship with Jesus had happened, marrying Leslie and having six children, going to law school, engaging in ministry and on and on. I had received countless blessings, and I thought, "Well, if I am to go into an end of life process right now, I have lived a full life. I've experienced such wonderful events. God has done such amazing things."

I really had a feeling of "Wow! I'm okay! A sense of satisfaction and fulfillment came over me, and the sense that if I'm going to die now, I have lived a full life—a rich life. I had this feeling of faithfulness and joy, and I really did experience what I would describe as a supernatural peace—as Paul said, "the peace of God, which transcends all understanding."

That was a major event in that hospital stay. It marked a turning point when my attitude changed. Reviewing my past and seeing how God had been at work in my life also brought to mind Romans 8:28 (NIV), "And we know that in all things God works for the good of those who love him, who have been called according to his purpose."

I could see that He had used events to make a real difference in my life and to reveal Himself to me and to strengthen our relationship and to show me His love. I was able to see those points in my life when God had shown His hand, and I thought, "It is so clear—so evident—that He has loved me in the past, then it must be true that He is loving me right now," and so as I sat in that hospital room, potentially facing the end of my life, it became clear to me that He was going to love me throughout the entire situation. Okay, I thought to myself, I'm in a hospital facing a rough cancer diagnosis and prognosis, but as I look back on my timeline and think about how blessed I have been, at some point in the future I may also look back at this and be thankful.

Don't get me wrong, I was not thankful for the cancer, nor will I ever be, but I was thankful even then of being able to sense God's presence and see Him working in my life. He had not abandoned me. He was with me, and up until that amazing peace came over me, I had taken my eyes off of that fact—that truth.

That was when I saw the power that can come from being thankful in all circumstances. It got me up out of my bed, and it got me doing the hard work of recovery, even though it was a struggle, and I didn't feel like it. It helped me live for the day. It removed the hopelessness and turned it into hope: a certainty that God was in charge of my life. Recently I heard a definition for fear that resonated with me —fear is to envision a future without God's grace, mercy and presence. Even though my physical survival prospect looked bleak (about 5% survival for metastatic urothelial bladder cancer), I did not have to fear, and instead I could enjoy hope —hope that God would partner with me no matter what came my way.

It's really all about surrender and trust that He really is a God of Love and has my best interests in mind. More than anything, that's what I learned. To surrender meant to give God control in my situation. It meant that I could let go and accept that He is in charge and has my best interests at heart. Did I really believe that? Did I really believe that He had a plan and a purpose in my bleak medical situation? It boiled down to the intimate relationship that I had with Jesus. I knew Him as my Higher Power — as my refuge and strength, my rescuer and healer. Yes, I could trust Him because He was worthy of my trust.

Making a list of what you are grateful for can make all the difference in your attitude and outlook. I know this because I've seen it happen with others. For example, a guy I sponsor was going through a divorce, and it was really hard for him. I was talking about it with him, and I said, "I've got some homework for you to do before the next time we talk. Write down ten things you're grateful for."

He did that, and it helped him. It helped him I think because it took his eyes off of the hurt that he was feeling in his life right then. It wasn't because he went into denial about his hurt, but being thankful caused him to look at all the other things that had happened in his life, and how God had used all these things for good. Once he realized that, he was able to see how God would eventually use what was going on now for good as well.

For me, having an "attitude of gratitude" was a game-changer.

In addition to gratitude, another concept that I believe God wanted me to wrestle with was hope. I have read and reread parts of my journal and the 23 truths that God gave me. Not long after that surgery on November 2, 2015 and the recovery, I contacted one of my friends who had terminal cancer. My friend Don was homebound and dealing with throat cancer. Don could no longer speak so he wrote down on his pad, "How was your surgery and recovery?" I have to say that I was still processing the entire experience. I still felt the trauma from it all — the surgery, recovery and prognosis. I felt raw and broken. Yet I also felt God's hand and His overwhelming presence. There was no doubt in my heart and spirit: He is my rock, refuge and strength — He was life itself. In that living room with my dying friend and his wife Cindy, I did not know what else to do but take out my journal and read from it — word for word. As I read, Don and Cindy listened and cried. I knew they could totally relate to what I had processed—the despair, anger and depression—yet the truths, God's presence, and a surrendered path through the cancer illness. Don and Cindy were walking in faith with their Lord and Savior. About a week after I read the journal to them, Don passed into glory. It was my pleasure and privilege to give a eulogy at his memorial service.

One more word about Don. At the memorial service, Don and Cindy's son mentioned a unique memory to me that I would like to share. It would be helpful for the reader to understand that to me Don was a very logical no nonsense, accounting type of guy. He would only deal with facts in a sincere and humble way. Don's son told me that as Don was still lucid yet very close to passing, he wrote on his pad, "I see Jesus." I will leave it at that but I have no doubt in my mind that Don saw glory as he was in the process of transitioning. You might want to read about the disciple Stephen's death in Acts 7:54-8:2 where he spoke about seeing Jesus and going to be with Him.

After I read my journal to Don and Cindy, I was asked to read it to a men's group in a local church. Not long after that, I was asked to read my journal word for word in a church service at a different local church. It cracks me up now as I think about the scene—I sat in front of the church and simply read from the journal. It took about an hour. I have been speaking in many churches and events since that time, and when I think about me just sitting there and reading, I am amazed at how gracious and loving those congregants were. And yet, I received many heartfelt responses from people who'd been impacted by what I'd written. I knew that God was doing some important work through my pain. He was using my pain and suffering to speak not only to me but to others as well. Even though it was devastating, my pain was not being wasted. I had surrendered it and my life to Jesus in trust, and He was using the journey to refine and build me up, and to speak truths into my life and into the lives of others.

My journal records my thoughts about hope, and how I processed the concept of hope in the hospital. I read these words from 1 Corinthians 13:13 (NIV): "And now these three remain: faith, hope and love. But the greatest of these is love." Those words struck me. I knew something about love and faith, not so much about hope.

Concerning love, most Christians are familiar with 1 Corinthians 13, which contains Paul's words about love. As a reminder, here are verses four and five (NIV): "Love is patient, love is kind. It does not envy, it does not boast, it is not proud. It does not dishonor others, it is not self-seeking, it is not easily angered, it keeps no record of wrongs."

God is love as love is defined above. That's how God loves us.

Faith also has many well-known definitions. Hebrews 11:1 (NIV) says, "Now faith is confidence in what we hope for and assurance about what we do not see." Faith is an inner conviction we have that I believe is based on a relationship with the Lord. It's something one feels in the heart, the spirit, and the soul, the feeling that what God has said is true—that we can trust Him. We go to Jesus in prayer because He is who He says He is, and we can have faith that whatever answer He gives will be in our best interests.

Earlier in this book, I mentioned a scene in Luke 8 where Jesus calms a perilous storm as he and the disciples were in a boat. The disciples believed that they were going to perish, and yet Jesus calmed the storm. After He calmed the storm and while still in the boat, Jesus looked back at His disciples and asked, "Where is your faith?" In other words, why don't you trust me? Also, Jesus explicitly mentions that it is not the quantity of faith that is necessary, that in fact one's faith may only be the size of a mustard seed (Luke 17:6 NIV). For me, faith is built on a foundation of Scripture and is exercised in the context of trust and dependence on Him.

Now let's consider the third concept, Hope, and how hope has provided meaning and purpose to my struggle. Romans 15:13 (NIV) says "May the God of hope fill you with all joy and peace as you trust in him, so that you may overflow with hope by the power of the Holy Spirit." Other translations also emphasize that we are to abound in hope.

It's essential, by the way, to understand that the word "hope" as it is used in the Bible does not have the connotation of "wishful thinking" that it has today. The original meaning infused in the Biblical word "hope" is a sense of trust—an expectation. In other words, "hope" as used in the Biblical sense is not "wishing" something would happen. It is waiting and *expecting* it to happen. There is "certainty" contained in the meaning of the word. Romans 8:24-25 (NIV) mentions that hope that is seen is no hope at all. That is not what hope is about. Hope is about a future event we have not yet experienced but we know will happen. There is no doubt attached to it.

Hope becomes possible by faith in a living God who can be trusted to keep His promises. Faith comes first, then hope. It becomes a joyful expectation that what he promises will come true. In the Bible, Abraham was promised to be the father of many nations by God, yet he and his wife did not have a son. It is said that Abraham was 75 years old when God promised him a son, and yet he did not have his son, Isaac until he was 100 years old. He and his wife Sarah were beyond childbearing years. Against all odds, by hope, Abraham believed that a son would be born, even though he saw no evidence that it was going to happen. Romans 4:18 (NIV) states that "against all hope, Abraham in hope believed and so became the father of many nations, just as it had been said to him, 'So shall your offspring be.'"

What did I have hope for at that time in my journey in the hospital?

I recorded in it the following:

1. Eternity; 2. Sharing in God's glory; 3. More future blessings; 4. Ultimate healing; 5. The constant presence of Jesus; and 6. His will being worked out in my life as I trust and depend on Him.

There is always room for hope. I have seen God do amazing things in my life and others. Just the other day, I was seeing my surgeon who scheduled a deep cystoscopy in the Operating Room. He has done several on me. Under general anesthesia, he scopes my entire urinary system to change stents, look for cancer and at times he lasers cancer and flushes my system with a liquid chemotherapy. However, he has told me that the next time he does this, he also plans to record what he does to my urinary system on video. My surgeon has another presentation coming up in Europe, and his contacts around the world keep asking him, "How is Peter." He told me once again, "You are a miracle! You should not be alive. You are an anomaly."

Well Praise God for anomalies. He can do whatever He wants. God can do anything. No matter what happens in my cancer journey, I intend and will endeavor to surrender and trust in Him—to abound in the God of all hope. More on my journey in cancer and my current state is coming in the next chapter as I enter the 15th year of my journey.

Chapter Six
My Journey Continues

Gratitude and hope—in the Biblical sense of "hope"—brought me out of the dark pit of depression I was in after the 2015 surgery. I was able to get out of bed, walk, do my rounds, and I began talking with others—reengaging with the world and doing the hard work of recovery. But, as mentioned at the end of Chapter Four, even though Dr. Grasso and the other surgeons had removed all the cancer they could see during that surgery, they believed there must have still been cancer cells in me that they had missed. Dr. Grasso wanted me to have chemo, but as you also know, I was turned down by the oncologists at Yale, Sloan, and Phelps because there was not clear evidence of cancer, and chemotherapy would have destroyed what little kidney function I had left. This put me into a kind of limbo state. Dr. Grasso knew I needed chemo, but no one would give it to me.

As was also mentioned at the end of Chapter Four, in May of 2016 I had a PET scan that lit up a couple of lymph nodes. I had a biopsy that required a seven-inch incision, three-hours of surgery, and a night in the ICU, but the pathology came back negative for cancer. Nevertheless, for more than a year following the 2015 surgery, I experienced a good deal of fatigue. Because I lacked energy, I struggled with work and with all of the other things I was involved for that entire time.

In February 2017, right around Valentine's Day, I had a regular office visit with Dr. Grasso. As I always did at those visits, I gave him a urine sample, and it turned out there was a lot going on in it, including the presence of blood. He admitted me into the hospital right then. When the pathology came back, it showed there were cancer cells present as well.

The next day, I had a PET scan, and Dr. Grasso went in under general anesthesia with a scope and found several tumors. One in my neobladder was the size of a tennis ball. He took biopsies and had them rushed to Lenox Hill Hospital to have them analyzed by a pathologist he trusted. I remained in the hospital, and on the third day, we got the news.

My brother Paul was with me when my oncologist and Dr. Grasso came into my room. They were teary eyed. Then, Dr. Grasso's fellow—a doctor who worked under him that I knew well came in, and he was actually crying.

Dr. Grasso and the oncologist came to me. They laid hands on me and said the cancer was all throughout my urinary system. They also said the PET scan indicated it was outside that immediate area as well, although still within the pelvic region. The somber and gloomy sense was pervasive, indicating, "This was it—the end—my demise was coming. It was only a matter of time." Dr. Grasso confirmed this when he told me he wanted me to go home, quit work, and go on disability.

As I look back, that moment is somewhat of a blur, but my brother tells me I looked at Dr. Grasso and said, "Dr. Grasso, you don't have to worry about me because I have a relationship with my Lord. I know exactly what's going to happen to me." Frankly, I don't recall saying exactly that, but I do remember telling him I had a strong relationship with the Lord, that the situation was in His hands, and whatever happens will be His will for me.

Dr. Grasso told me he had spoken with Dr. Herr at Sloan Kettering and that in more than thirty years of practice, this would only be the fourth time he'd seen or heard of a tumor in a neobladder. Dr. Herr advised Dr. Grasso to send me home and call hospice. Dr. Grasso said he wasn't ready yet to "throw in the towel," that he was going to strategize about what to do and what could be done.

I have to give special kudos to Dr. Grasso and say that he has gone well above and beyond what any doctor would be expected to do. He has done whatever was in my best interest throughout this entire journey—through countless procedures and office visits. I believe God called him specifically to aid me on my cancer journey.

Later, in my hospital bed, I turned to the Lord and said, "I surrender and trust you Lord. If this is my time to come to be with You, then Lord, just travel with me."

I knew that He would, and I also began watching videos about near death experiences, and I read a book entitled, *Imagine Heaven: Near-Death Experiences, God's Promises, and the Exhilarating Future That Awaits You* by John Burke. I have to say I found the videos and this book to be a comfort. It's a fact that there have been literally thousands of accounts of near death experiences given by people who have been clinically dead for a short time and then resuscitated or revived spontaneously. They typically have memories of vivid sensory imagery, and an extremely clear memory of what they experienced. Often they describe what they experienced as seeming "more real" than their everyday lives. The common features of NDEs can be categorized as changes in thinking, changes in emotional state, as well as paranormal and otherworldly features.

I learned from John Burke's book that the Apostle Paul apparently had a near death experience. These verses from Acts 14:19-20 (NIV) may refer to the event that precipitated it:

> *Then some Jews came from Antioch and Iconium and won the crowd over. They stoned Paul and dragged him outside the city, thinking he was dead. But after the disciples had gathered around him, he got up and went back into the city. The next day he and Barnabas left for Derbe.*

And it seems likely that Paul may be relating what he may have experienced in this passage from 2 Corinthians 12:2-4 (NIV):

I know a man in Christ who fourteen years ago was caught up to the third heaven. Whether it was in the body or out of the body I do not know—God knows. And I know that this man—whether in the body or apart from the body I do not know, but God knows— was caught up to paradise and heard inexpressible things, things that no one is permitted to tell.

John Burke's book contains a number of descriptions by near death survivors of heaven, and what they experienced there, and so if you are interested, I urge you to read his book. To give you a taste, I will quote a portion of one of them here. It was told by George Ritchie (1923-2007) who, as a young soldier in World War Two, died of pneumonia at Camp Barkley, Texas. According to reports, Ritchie was dead for nine minutes before coming back to life. He said that once he realized he was dead, the light in the room started to grow brighter and brighter:

I stared in astonishment as the brightness increased, coming from nowhere, seeming to shine everywhere at once. . . . It was impossibly bright: it was like a millions welder's lamps all blazing at once. And right in the middle of my amazement came a prosaic thought probably born of some biology lecture back at the university: "I'm glad I don't have physical eyes at the moment," I thought. "This would destroy my retina in a tenth of a second."

No, I corrected myself, not the light.

He.

He would be too bright to look at. For now I saw that it was not the light but a Man who had entered the room, or rather, a Man made out of light. . . .

The instant I perceived Him, a command formed itself in my mind. "Stand up!" The words came from inside me, yet they had an authority my mere thoughts had never had. I got to my feet, and as I did came the stupendous certainty: You are in the presence of the Son of God.

George thought about Jesus, the Son of God, whom he had learned about in Sunday school—gentle, meek, kind of a weakling. But this person was Power itself fused together with an unconditional love that overwhelmed him.

An astonishing love. A love beyond my wildest imagining. This love knew every unlovable thing about me—the quarrels with my stepmother, my explosive temper, the sex thoughts I could never control, every mean, selfish thought and action since the day I was born—and accepted and loved me just the same.

When I say He knew everything about me, this was simply an observable fact, for into that room along with His radiant presence—simultaneously, though in telling about it I have to describe them one by one—had also entered every single episode of my entire life. Everything that had ever happened to me was simply there, in full view, contemporary and current, all seemingly taking place at that moment.

How this was possible I did not know. . . .

. . . Transfixed, I stared at myself standing at the blackboard in a third-grade spelling class. Receiving my Eagle badge in front of my scout troop. Wheeling Papa Dabney onto the verandah at Moss Side. . . .

There were other scenes, hundreds, thousands, all illuminated by that searing Light, in an existence where time seemed to have ceased. It would have taken weeks of ordinary time. . . .

Every detail of twenty years of living was there to be looked at. . . .

"What have you done with your life to show Me?"

The question, like everything else proceeding from Him, had to do with love. How much have you

*loved with your life? Have you loved others as I am
loving you? Totally? Unconditionally?*
  *. . . Why, I had not known love like this was pos-
sible. Someone should have told me, I thought in-
dignantly! A fine time to discover what life was all
about. . .*
  "I did tell you."
  *But how? Still wanting to justify myself. How
could He have told me and I not have heard?*
  "I told you by the life I lived. I told you by the
death I died. And, if you keep your eyes on Me, you
will see more."

Imagine, being in the presence of Jesus. It's not surprising that near death survivors frequently report changes in
attitudes, beliefs, and values, and that these changes do not
seem to fade over time. They report overwhelmingly that
they are more spiritual because of their experience, that they
have more compassion, a greater desire to help others, a
greater appreciation for life as well as a stronger sense of
meaning and purpose in life. This was certainly true of
George Ritchie. After he was revived and had recovered
from pneumonia, he went on to become a medical doctor
and a psychiatrist and to serve others in a number of positions, including as president of the Richmond (Virginia)
Academy of General Practice; chairman of the Department

of Psychiatry of Towers Hospital; and the founder and president of the Universal Youth Corps.

His story and others helped me prepare mentally for an end of life process. I figured I had probably six months to a year to live. As I'm sure you can imagine, I began thinking seriously about how I wanted to spend the final six months or so of my life. What was really and truly important to me? There's nothing more compelling than a diagnosis like the one I'd had to cause a person to ask, "In my life, where does the rubber meet the road? What is truly important to me?"

I thought, do I want to travel more? Do I want to buy a fast car? Do I want to live life on the edge? What do I want?

What came to me was, "I want to leave a legacy for my children and family, and I want to live out each day however the Lord wants me to live it." I put Him in total charge of my end-of-life journey—I surrender and trust in Him. Whatever the Lord had in store for me, I was going to live in that.

After four days in the hospital, I went home, and I wrote letters to Leslie and to each of my kids. I gave Leslie hers, and I still have the letters to my kids.

I wrote in those letters what I felt in my heart about each of them—what I felt when they were born and growing up. It wasn't so much what each one did or said, I wrote about how I felt about each one—what my heart had to say. It took me a week to write each one of those letters because it was such a struggle. It was my way of saying goodbye, my way of paying tribute to each one. They were like the letter I wrote to my mom before she died. I told each child about the special characteristics and attributes I saw in each one, and that I love, and I gave them each a Bible verse and encouraged them in their walks in life.

Then I sealed the envelopes.

I also continued with Celebrate Recovery® and the cancer support group at my church, and I started doing videos, which I based on the Serenity Prayer. I don't recall exactly how many it took, but I used that prayer because it embodies how I would like to live my life. I believe the Serenity Prayer reveals a pathway to having a relationship with God, and to having peace and joy in life. I did the videos for my kids but I also posted them on YouTube. You can access them by putting "Peter Scalzo channel" in the search feature on YouTube.

Not long after that mid-February 2017 event in the hospital, the elders and pastors of my church put on an all-night prayer vigil for me in the prayer room, and about 20 people came. I feel compelled to say that so many Christians, pastors, and churches have prayed over me during the years of my journey, that I am so very appreciative to all of them and to everyone who has expressed love to me in that way.

The all-night vigil was particularly special. We started out with some worship, communion, and then we went to times of prayer. I was there until about five o'clock in the morning.

There were two significant questions asked of me that night. One was, "Peter, do you really want to be healed?" I hesitated long enough before answering that it raised a question in my mind. I knew I had not stopped fighting, but I did have to wonder if I was ready to go and be with the Lord.

It wasn't the first time the question had been raised in my mind. People had said before that I didn't have to have cancer in order to feel close to the God. Apparently, they suspected that, perhaps subconsciously, I wanted the cancer and didn't want to be healed because it brought me closer to Him. Frankly, I don't think that was the case, but even so, that night that I made a decision. I said to the Lord, "My life is in your hands, but I'm asking you to heal me. I want to be healed."

Of course, I have always asked Him to heal me—to put cancer in my rearview mirror—but that night at that all-night session, I really, truly, without question wanted to be healed. Of course, I would be okay with however it went—content with whatever was God's plan—whether He was going to heal me or take me home.

The second significant thing that happened was that an elder looked at me, and said with a sense of urgency, "Peter, are you doing *everything* you can? *Everything?*"

The message came loud and clear, and I said, "No, I am not. I am not going to chase cancer cures. I'm not going to fly around the world, go to Mexico or Europe, or wherever—to chase cancer cures. I will do what is reasonable medically—as God leads me. But I am totally in God's hands, and I am not frantic."

It was clear to me that if I were doing that sort of thing—chasing the next fad cancer cure—it would be out of fear, and that's not how I wanted to operate.

I said to those present, "My body is broken and poured out before you. I am resigned to what Jesus wants in this situation. I am going to live for Him, and I'm going to do what brings me life, and that means spending time with my children and allowing Jesus to work in me and through me."

It was a very significant night for me.

Around the same time the prayer vigil took place something incredible happened. You might even call it a miracle. In 2016, six months before I would need it, the FDA had fast-tracked and approved an immunotherapy drug called "Tecentriq" that was specifically intended for metastatic bladder cancer. The timing of the development of such a drug and that the FDA had fast-tracked it was really quite something when you think about it. The more prevalent types of cancer, such as lung cancer and breast cancer, naturally get more research. High-grade urothelial bladder cancer—which I have—is very aggressive. It is also fairly rare, and so there had not been much research done on it. Tecentriq was the first such drug, and in addition to the timing of its release, my insurance covered most of the cost. The drug company covered the rest because they wanted people to try it.

And so I started on Tecentriq only a few weeks following the hospital stay, biopsy, and the tearful news delivered by Dr. Grasso.

Tecentriq is a checkpoint inhibitor. The theory behind it is that T-cells in the body act like agents at a TSA checkpoint in an airport to stop the bad guys from getting through. In my case, my T-cells were letting the cancer cells live. It was discovered that there's a protein called a PD-L1 that wraps itself around and camouflages the cancer cells. Tecentriq was designed to break apart the PD-L1 so that the T-cells could attack and kill the cancer cells.

The drug was administered in a chemotherapy infusion suite every three weeks. The actual infusion is an I.V. drip that only takes about thirty minutes, but when you have chemo, you go to your oncologist and have your blood tested because they want to see your white blood cell count. If the white blood cell count is too low, they cannot administer the chemo. So you have to get approval from the blood work first before you can receive the chemotherapy. Of course, I wasn't having chemotherapy; I was having immunotherapy. But because immunotherapy was so new at the time, the same protocol applied even though it really didn't make sense because it was my immune system that was going to go after the cancer.

We didn't know whether or not immunotherapy was working, but after about three months, Dr. Grasso did a cystoscopy in his office. I could see what was happening on a screen. The tumor in my bladder looked like a mushroom attached to the wall on one side. It looked big on the screen.

I said, "That looks big."

He said, "Yes, but it has shrunk from the side of a tennis ball to the size of a golf ball!" He was really excited about the progress and said, "Let's continue doing what we are doing."

Three months after that, I went to see Dr. Grasso again for a cystoscopy. As soon as he put the scope in, he leaned back and screamed, "It's gone! I can't believe it! The tumor is gone!"

I said, "Wow, immunotherapy!"

He said, "Immunotherapy, nothing. God is good! This is amazing!"

Something very significant had happened. It was a miracle, and I don't think there are any second-rate miracles. When we experience healing, whether it's within or outside the medical community, it is God at work.

That's when I thought about the story in Scripture when Jesus heals ten lepers and only one comes back to thank Jesus for that healing, and I certainly wanted to do the same. I publically thanked Jesus for the healing. This was a major event in the war against cancer in my body.

I continued to have infusions every three weeks, as well as PET scans and doctor's appointments, and there was no evidence of cancer again until December 2018. That blew the doctors away. I was seemingly cancer free for almost 22 months, although I did have some side effects, such as fatigue, rashes, and some arthritic issues.

In December 2018 a PET scan showed a one-inch tumor in my pelvic area next to my neobladder. Dr. Grasso put me under general anesthesia, went inside and found cancer in a kidney, a ureter, and the neobladder. He lasered the cancer and gave me a chemo rinse—a chemotherapy that kills cancer on contact. He repeated that procedure two more times in December and January, and put stents in my ureters to facilitate the urine flow. He also told me I needed a new immunotherapy drug. Unfortunately there weren't many options.

During the first week in January 2019, an intervention radiologist went in under general anesthesia and froze the one-inch tumor. He thought that he got 99 percent of it. After that we switched to Keytruda, which is another immunotherapy drug. Instead of targeting the PD-L1 protein with Tecentriq, which didn't seem to be working anymore, Keytruda targets the PD-1 protein, which is the one wrapped around my T-1 cells.

I had another PET scan in May 2019, and the one-inch tumor that the doctor thought he had taken care of was now two and a half inches in size. Dr. Grasso said he could not go in and removed it surgically because there was too much scar tissue, and so for a while I didn't know if there was a way to tackle this tumor. Then Dr. Grasso sent me to see a radiation oncologist in lower Manhattan, who normally works on heads and necks using very precisely targeted radiation, which he is able to direct using information from a series of CT scans. He has a physicist feed the parameters into a computer in order to pinpoint the radiation. Dr. Grasso wanted me to see this particular therapist because he was concerned that if it were not precisely targeted, the radiation would damage my bowel and neobladder.

As of this writing I have just completed five weeks of intensive radiation therapy, Monday through Friday, five days a week. I experienced fatigue as well as some bowel and neobladder issues, but after three weeks, the tumor had been reduced by more than half. The tumor is still there, and as of now, the status of it is unknown, but it has been hit with as many "rads" as possible, and I am optimistic that for now at least the cancer is under control.

Chapter Seven
Parting Thoughts

I am grateful and surprised to see where I am today. I am still in the center of an intense cancer journey, yet I am immersed in my personal faith recovery journey and my passions for volunteering in the spaces of recovery and cancer support. I spend quality time with my family and friends. I have more personal time now than I have ever had to meditate, to read and to enjoy my relationship with my Higher Power. My doctors are surprised I am alive. I know I am powerless over this journey. I have chosen, however, to walk into the pain and suffering of this journey with my Higher Power. I cannot do this on my own. I need Jesus. I also need my family. I need my friends. I need other people of faith. I need my recovery family, my support group, and my church family. I have seen the same therapist for years now. He has helped me process many issues in my life.

God has blessed me with an incredible medical team. Besides my skillful and caring doctors, I cannot say enough about the angel nurses that I have had. My hospital stays have been long and painful, and yet I have met so many wonderful and caring people who work in hospitals and medical offices. I know God has called many of them into what they do. I am so thankful for Dr. Herr and the folks at Memorial Sloan Kettering. I am so thankful for my oncologist, Dr. Anna Komorowski at Phelp's Memorial Hospital. She is smart and compassionate. I have had a long relationship with Dr. Michael Grasso and have seen him go above and beyond what I would ever expect. It has been a horrific journey, and yet so fulfilling at times. I have seen God perform a healing miracle in my body. I have felt the raw terror of cancer diagnoses and an end of life prognosis. I have travelled the end-of-life journey with many others.

It's so tempting to want to assume control over my journey. When I am in that place, I struggle with issues such as fear and anxiety. I have gone through times of dealing with anger and resentment. I have had doubts and felt hopelessness. Many times I just want the journey to be over. I want to move on with my life. Yet, I am forced to deal with the reality of treatments, tests, procedures, and everything that comes with having a life threatening illness. For me, I have gained peace, comfort and even joy by dwelling in a place of surrender and trust.

One day I was discussing with the Lord what surrender really means for my life. I talked about surrendering every aspect of my life to Him: relationships, finances, children, career, my cancer journey, health, and so forth. I believe the message I received from Him is that surrender for me means giving God sovereignty over that issue. It is a process and a struggle. When I do make the choice to surrender to God, it does not mean, however, that I can walk away from, or turn my back on decisions to be made. What it does mean is that in each situation I will endeavor to turn my will and the situation over to the Lord for His guidance and His will to be done. For example, He has charge or sovereignty over my health and my cancer journey, but I still have to look to Him for input on decisions to be made along the way. In other words, what hospital and doctors to use, what meds to take, what diet and nutrition I should be on, and so forth. But even though I have those types of decisions to make, I look to the Lord for His presence, His guidance, courage, comfort and His peace.

Ultimately, however, He is in control.

There usually is a threshold question for me: do I really and truly trust that He will do whatever is in my best interest? For example, can I really trust the Lord with all the aspects of the cancer journey, including life itself? Do I trust Jesus with my life? Is He worthy of my trust? Do I really believe that He causes all things to work together for good? Do I believe that when I am on the operating table, when I am getting news of metastatic cancer, or when I am told to call hospice? Is God still good in the face of devastation?

Yes, I believe He is. I have come to trust God. He is good. God is my refuge and strength. He knows my very thoughts and every hair on my head. There have been times in my journey when I have been so broken in every way, that all I could muster was a weak attempt to say "Jesus." I have felt so alone and depressed at times. And yet it was always God who showed up. It may have been a greeting card, a visit, a special phone call, a prayer, a song, or whatever. I have felt Him in such profound ways—ways I will never forget. I know that Jesus is real. I am so appreciative.

One day in the hospital after my 2015 surgery—which I wrote about in Chapter Four—I was still on life support with water and nutrition coming to me through an I.V. I had no bowel function and was dependent on the other methods of support as well. As you recall, I told the Lord how disappointed I was. I told Him that He could heal me right then and there—that I could walk out of that hospital bed.

It was then that I heard His voice in my heart and in spirit:

Will you surrender and trust Me, even in this situation? Do you believe that I have your best interests at heart and that I have a plan and purpose in this? Your life is in my hands.

At that point, sitting in my bed, I resigned myself again, and I surrendered everything to the God who loves and partners with me. He had allowed this situation to happen. I accepted this hardship, and when I did, I experienced the Lord's wonderful peace, comfort and love.

People say that peace is so very evident in my life. That is not me—it is the God of peace in me. The Lord has taken my anxiety and fear on and given me peace and comfort—even in the midst of the cancer storm.

It's not about me manipulating God into getting Him to do what I want him to do, saying something like, "Okay, God, you have to heal me today." No, it's that I need to surrender to what God is doing and actually trust that He's a good and loving Father. For some of us, that it is a concept we struggle to accept. We may have had such negative experiences in life with parents or whatever authority is responsible for us. There could have been abuse or abandonment. I can see how that experience could influence how someone might view a sovereign Higher Power. I have chosen to view God with a "healed" lens. My understanding of Him has been shaped by the Scriptures and through my relationship with Jesus. I do my best to navigate the Bible with the help of the Holy Spirit and others. I am on a faith journey just like many of us are—seeking meaning and purpose in our lives, and I have found meaning and purpose.

Many people ask how I am able to survive emotionally and spiritually in my journey. Often, I feel as though I have one foot in eternity, and the other on this earth. I would never have chosen this path I'm on, but I am amazed at what God has done in my life, and what He has done for others as a result of my journey.

Paul says in 1 Corinthians 6:19-20 (NIV):

Do you not know that your bodies are temples of the Holy Spirit, who is in you, whom you have received from God? You are not your own; you were bought at a price. Therefore honor God with your bodies.

God owns my body—so why did I get cancer? It may have happened because of genetics or simply from living in a broken world where cancer is endemic. Perhaps it was Satan's work. I don't know how the cancer happened. I don't think God caused it, but I do believe He allowed it, just as He allowed Job to suffer and Paul to have a thorn in his side. God knew that the cancer was going to happen, and he allowed it to happen. He could have stopped it, but He said, "No, I am going to allow my son and citizen, Peter, whom I love and own, to go through a cancer journey." He did so because He had a purpose and a plan, and He knew that cancer would bring me closer to Him. The cancer didn't happen because God was distracted, took His eye off the ball and didn't notice what was going on. That simply doesn't happen. As it says in Psalm 139:7-12 (NIV):

Where can I go from your Spirit? Where can I flee from your presence? If I go up to the heavens, you are there; if I make my bed in the depths, you are there. If I rise on the wings of the dawn, if I settle on

the far side of the sea, even there your hand will
guide me, your right hand will hold me fast. If I say,
"Surely the darkness will hide me and the light be-
come night around me," even the darkness will not
be dark to you; the night will shine like the day, for
darkness is as light to you.

God is constantly thinking about each one of us. As David wrote, also in Psalm 139:4 (NIV), "Before a word is on my tongue you, Lord, know it completely." And also in Psalm 139: 17 (NLT), "How precious are your thoughts about me, O God. They cannot be numbered." In other words, God is not aloof. He knows what's going on in each of our lives. For some people that may be pretty unnerving, especially if they think of God as a strict parent that is constantly judging us, and that He has a wagging finger pointed at us for our transgressions. But I don't believe that concept is anything close to what God is really like. He doesn't punish us. What He does is mold and fashion us, and He does so because he knows that when we are broken and powerless, we have the opportunity to turn our lives and will over to Him. King David wrote in Psalm 34:18 (NIV) "The Lord is close to the brokenhearted and saves those who are crushed in spirit." He also wrote Psalm 51:16-17 (NIV) "You do not delight in sacrifice, or I would bring it; you do not take pleasure in burnt offerings. My sacrifice, O God, is a broken spirit; a broken and contrite heart you, God, will not despise." I experience such peace, comfort and joy when I acknowledge my brokenness before Him—that I need my Higher Power and am dependent on Him, like a little child. God is in control, not me, and He has my best interests at heart.

You may know Joni Eareckson Tada. She is a Christian author, speaker, cancer survivor, radio host and founder of Joni & Friends, an organization "accelerating Christian ministry in the disability community." In 1967 at age 17, Joni dove into the water, broke her spine and became a quadriplegic. She speaks extensively about her journey into suicidal thoughts, anger, depression and doubts about God. What I love about her journey is her understanding and recognition of what God can do in pain and suffering. Here are a few statements she has made:

"Sometimes God allows what he hates to accomplish what he loves."
— Joni Eareckson Tada, The God I Love

" . . . we will stand amazed to see the topside of the tapestry and how God beautifully embroidered each circumstance into a pattern for our good and His glory."
— Joni Eareckson Tada

"Suffering provides the gym equipment on which
my faith can be exercised."
— Joni Eareckson Tada, *Suffering: Making Sense
of Suffering 5pk*

For many of us, pain is an invitation to change. We have a choice to make. Understanding God's purpose and plan in pain and suffering can help us see how God can work for good in all things. An amazing concept on trials is presented by James in Scripture. In James 1:2-4 (NIV) he writes, "Consider it pure joy, my brothers and sisters, whenever you face trials of many kinds, because you know that the testing of your faith produces perseverance. Let perseverance finish its work so that you may be mature and complete, not lacking anything."

James tells us to consider trials to be pure joy. How could that possibly be?

James then presents a process, and I know from what he writes that if I walk into and through my cancer journey in surrender and trust, I will persevere through it.

The journey has not been easy for me. I am so very tired of cancer. Yet I know that I have no control over it. I have asked the Lord to give me the serenity or peace to accept those things that I cannot change—cancer, in other words.

It seems as though I am constantly in the cancer journey, and yet I continue to walk—to move forward—through and because of my relationship with Jesus. I am honest and intimate with Him, and He provides me with peace and joy. Therefore, I am able to persevere and endure.

The verses in James tell me that I will be mature and complete. To me that means that maturity and completeness have to do with total reliance on Jesus. I can't do this journey, but He can do it in me, and through me.

Later in James, the text talks about Job as a man who is blessed because he persevered or endured during his trials. James 5:11 says "As you know, we count as blessed those who have persevered. You have heard of Job's perseverance and have seen what the Lord finally brought about. The Lord is full of compassion and mercy."

Job is a man in the Bible who suffered great losses. His children died, his business was lost, and he suffered from painful sores all over his body. His wife told him to "curse God and die." What Job didn't know was that God had allowed Satan to bring all those trials on him. Job became very depressed and questioned what was happening to him. He cursed the day he was born. God responded to Job but did not explain why the trials had come. God's message was, "Surrender and trust, I am in charge."

Even though Job experienced depression and other feelings, he was praised for persevering, and for having patience in his suffering. I am grateful for what God can provide in the trial of my cancer journey—perseverance. I'll say it again. The serenity prayer has a message that provides solid advice and perspective, "Living one day at a time, enjoying one moment at a time, accepting hardship as a pathway to peace." In addition, there is an interesting concept introduced in Scripture concerning Jesus. Hebrews 5:8 (NIV) tells us, "Son though he was, he learned obedience from what he suffered." There was something very unique about Jesus and His humanity that came about because He suffered, and I believe God can use pain and suffering the same way in our lives.

We may not realize it, but whether or not we benefit is a choice that is ours to make. As Jesus said in John 10:10 (NIV), "The thief comes only to steal and kill and destroy; I have come that they may have life, and have it to the full." I believe in speaking life into the cancer journey, no matter how dark or bleak it may seem at times. When I accepted that God had a purpose and a plan in my journey, I knew He carried me along. I could not handle the overwhelming devastation of a bleak cancer diagnosis. But Jesus could handle it, and He does handle it. It is not me, but Christ in me and through me. Even in a cancer journey, Jesus can deliver life, and He does deliver it. He has provided healing, joy, comfort and peace to me when it seemed to make no sense at all.

Jesus is a life-giver. I think it is the same truth that Paul talks about in Philippians 4:12-13 when he wrote, "I know what it is to be in need, and I know what it is to have plenty. I have learned the secret of being content in any and every situation, whether well fed or hungry, whether living in plenty or in want. I can do all this through him who gives me strength."

I, too, can actually be content even in an intense cancer journey. Only through an intimate and dependent relationship with Him can I experience strength and life. It is the same concept the Apostle Paul communicates in Galatians 2:20 when he says that he has been crucified with Christ and that Christ lives in and through him.

And there is something else I want you to know. My exit strategy has been of critical importance to me during my journey. As I will explain, it is possible for me to cling to my exit strategy because of my worldview, which entails a belief that is a tremendous source of comfort.

It seems to me we all have a worldview whether or not we have thought about it and brought it out of our subconscious minds to examine it in the light of day. Worldviews typically have six to eight components, such as, where do we come from and how do we discern right and wrong? One of the biggest and most important components is, "What happens when we die?" If you are a Scientific Materialist, for example, the answer is, "Nothing." For a Scientific Materialist the body is like a robot and the brain is like a computer, and so, when the plug is pulled, that's it—lights out, *fini, kaput!*

If that's what you think, or you know someone who does, let me tell you that there's plenty of evidence showing that worldview is woefully incorrect. If you don't believe me, read my friend Stephen Hawley Martin's book, *How Science Reveals God: What Every Thinking Person Must Know.* It gives solid scientific evidence to support what I believe happens after death—a belief I have based on Scripture.

In the Old Testament, what happened after death was vague, but thankfully, Jesus cleared up the mystery. Trusting that what Scripture says is true—along with the accounts of near death experiences in John Burke's book—has made all the difference for me. If, for example, I'm in a hospital or doctor's office and get bad news, I find comfort in the knowledge of what's ultimately going to happen to me, and it's all good. These excerpts from Scripture tell the tale:

Philippians 1:21 (NIV)

For to me, to live is Christ and to die is gain.

1 Corinthians 15: 55- 57

"Where, O death, is your victory? Where, O death, is your sting?" The sting of death is sin, and the power of sin is the law. But thanks be to God! He gives us the victory through our Lord Jesus Christ.

John 11:25 - 27

Jesus said to her, "I am the resurrection and the life. The one who believes in me will live, even though they die; and whoever lives by believing in me will never die. Do you believe this?"

"Yes, Lord," she replied, "I believe that you are the Messiah, the Son of God, who is to come into the world."

2 Corinthians 5:8 (NIV):

We are confident, I say, and would prefer to be away from the body and at home with the Lord.

The verses above give me comfort, which raises a question I want to answer for those who may be interested. What's the best way in my view to comfort a friend or a loved one who has been diagnosed with cancer?

Having spent 15 years on this journey, I can tell you what has worked and what has not worked for me. This is my perspective. For example, I do not want to hear pat answers. I do however want to hear genuine words of comfort and optimism. There is always hope. I remember a long hospital stay and reading and re-reading cards and notes of encouragement. They were food to my weary soul.

I understand that cancer and an end of life prognosis and journey are very sad. I understand that people need to mourn and may need to do it at the bedside. But for me, I do not find it helpful for people to come and mourn or weep over me. I want to see life. I want to see people who are living life. I want to see normal life moving forward even though mine has been upended. By the way, there is always the possibility of a miracle—a situation that baffles the medical community. It has happened in my life. I have seen God do amazing things in the face of hopelessness.

In the hospital, I believe visits are welcome although there should be great sensitivity to people trying to recover. I appreciated short visits. I barely had enough energy to talk. I don't think visitors should feel pressure to say the "right thing." Recently I visited a 60 year old woman from my cancer support group who was just told that there was nothing more to do except to call hospice. I simply held her hand while she wept. I said nothing. Whenever I visit anyone dealing with a health issue, I always pray, "Lord, I can't do this but You can. I need You." Many times I sit and listen rather than offer anything. I have spent so many unique and wonderful times visiting people—simply listening and offering an encouraging word, or Scripture—but only when prompted.

It is not helpful to look for a cause or to try to find something to blame for the cancer. A cancer patient who's recently been diagnosed is suffering a loss—a traumatic loss of health and of life as he or she knew it. In dealing with that, they are going through a process that typically involves five stages. Not necessarily in this order, they are: 1) Denial and isolation, 2) anger, 3) bargaining, 4) depression, and eventually, 5) acceptance. Talking about causes and what's to blame is not helpful while that process is going on. What is helpful is to live in the moment—to get through the moment—and it's helpful during that time to be surrounded by people who are positive and upbeat.

There are times I have had to process a new cancer diagnosis. Recurrences are especially difficult. For me I need space. I need to run the prospect of sickness and perhaps death through my grid. I partner with Jesus. It is so very difficult. One day I asked the cancer support group at church: what is the most helpful place for you to be in to survive the cancer journey? They all said the same thing, "acceptance." Acceptance provides peace. Some people never arrive there. They get stuck in anger or depression, for example. I get it. I don't judge or condemn. It is a personal journey. It is a journey into trauma. There are times when I get flashbacks. I will be walking in a hospital or putting on shaving cream that has a particular smell, and I am transported back to my hospital room experiencing pain, nausea, despair or whatever was happening. I turn that image over to my Higher Power. I thank Him for delivering me. I look for the good. Acceptance is key. It is a process. It involves walking into the pain. Lord, grant me the serenity or peace to accept those things that I cannot change—living one day at a time, enjoying one moment at a time—accepting hardship as a pathway to peace.

What I need are people that give me strength and energy—encouragement. I don't usually want to hear about a new diet or new treatment. One can find anything on the internet these days. My personal belief is that cancer is a very complex disease. We are tempted to want to know why there is so much cancer. Cancer seems to have affected most families. When I have to explain the prevalence of cancer, I talk about things such as environmental factors, anxiety, stress, diet, the additives in foods, genetics and the immune system. I really don't know. There are too many rule breakers. I have met vegetarians, who are also marathoners, but have cancer. I have met people who smoked their entire lives and die in their 90's with no cancer. People look for a cause. How about the child that gets diagnosed? I have seen many children in cancer centers dealing with cancer. I know some people that believe a cure has been discovered but is being stifled by the medical or pharma industry so they can make more money. My experience has been dealing with caring medical professionals who would love to end cancer once and for all. I believe there are probably arguments to be made on all sides. The financial pressure that I have experienced from cancer has been overwhelming. Millions of dollars have been spent on my care over the years. Just since January of this year, with tests, procedures and treatments, around $475,000 has been spent on my care. That is unbelievable. I have not even experienced any major surgeries or hospital stays. There are some people in faith that believe a person is not healed due to a lack of faith or not praying the correct prayers. My advice is to please be sensitive. The person with cancer is really struggling. The person is overwhelmed. The person needs a loving touch, a gentle reminder of your love for him or her. The person needs encouragement—that we will get through this. I have been so saddened at times over the pain, suffering and utter losses. Many of my friends and family have died from cancer. Because of the circles I travel in, I am constantly confronted by the prospect of death. I have encouraged many people in their end of life process. And you know what? We will all experience death. Death is inevitable. I am amazed when I see a person of faith, traveling in love and acceptance, transition to glory. I have felt God's presence in the room. I have seen such peace and even joy. Yes, when we know Jesus and transition out of our bodies into His presence—Wow! Also, I have seen life come from death. I have seen family members turn their lives over to Jesus, and I have seen them gain a new perspective. What an impact our passing can have on the ones we love! For example, my mom taught me a lot in life. She also taught me how to transition into eternity with honesty, peace, acceptance and dignity. Mom struggled with dying. She was honest. Mom did not want to leave. She wanted to take care of dad and be with her children and grandchildren. In many ways, she was the glue of our family. Wherever she went, Mom would have her camera in hand to record the event. We had hundreds of pictures of us and our families because of Mom. She made life fun. Mom made holidays special. She made each person in the family feel special—a unique nickname, a listening and compassionate ear, a special meal. In her cancer journey, Mom clung to Jesus, and it showed. Mom was genuine. I appreciated her honesty and perspective. In the end of life process, Mom surrendered and trusted in her Higher Power: Jesus.

News flash—September 9, 2019: I just got back from a visit with Dr. Grasso. As you recall, I mentioned in Chapter Five that he was going to perform a deep cystoscopy on me in the Operating Room, and that he planned to record on video what he did to my urinary system because he has another presentation coming up in Europe. Perhaps you remember that his contacts around the world keep asking him, "How is Peter?" He plans to not only to tell them, but to show them. Well, under general anesthesia, he scoped my entire urinary system, changed stents, looked for cancer, and it was clean. He did not see any. For me, it does not get any better than that!

Some time ago, a malignant tumor that was removed from me was tested at Sloan Kettering for the number of genetic mutations that had been going on in it. Called "Tumor Mutation Burden," or TMB, the technique measures how many genetic mutations were happening with a measurement called, "TMBs per mega-base." What the test showed, however, is that I had a very high TMB. The normal/median for Sloan Kettering is 3.9 TMBs per mega-base, and for the type of bladder cancer I had, it is 8.8 TMBs per mega-base.

Mine was 29 TMBs.

In other words, mine was incredibly high—more than three times the norm. No doubt that's the reason cancer has been such a problem for me and has spread so fast. But according to my immunologist, it is also the reason immunotherapy has worked so well in my particular case. Apparently, once the immune system becomes invigorated, it targets all those genetic mutations. As the old saying goes, "Every cloud has a silver lining," or to put it in Scriptural terms, "And we know that in all things God works for the good of those who love him, who have been called according to his purpose." (Romans 8:28 NIV).

This brings up one more thing that I think needs to be said. Since I believe in and acknowledge a spiritual world in addition to this physical one that you and I now inhabit, the Scriptures as I understand them recognize not only the existence of heaven, but also the existence of hell—including Satan, the accuser, and demons. I began this book encouraging the reader to have a relationship with Jesus as a Higher Power. This may surprise you, having read this far, but I don't really consider myself to be a particularly religious person. For me, my life journey is completely integrated with a relationship with my Higher Power. I don't view that as the same thing as being religious. Nevertheless, I feel compelled to say this: Based on my understanding of the Bible, Jesus offers each and every one of us a choice to make concerning where we will spend eternity. Every one of us is going to have an existence in the afterlife, and I believe that existence will either be in heaven or in hell. So here's what I think needs to be said: Romans 10:19 (NIV) states that "If you declare with your mouth, 'Jesus is Lord,' and believe in your heart that God raised him from the dead, you will be saved."

Please understand that I do not wish to push my views on anyone. I love the 12 steps of recovery because they encourage the participant to have a Higher Power—to recognize that in many ways we are powerless and that our lives can be unmanageable. My opinion is that a life lived recognizing that one does not have all the answers, that we need help from a Higher Power, as well as from others, is a life lived in both humility and in abundance.

I believe that is true because it has been my experience. The bottom line is this: Life is not all about me, and I am not alone. I have an exit strategy for when the time comes for me to leave planet Earth. The same strategy allows me to have found meaning and abundance, humor, and tears while on my cancer journey. In 2017, I was told to go home—that it was all over. I asked myself—whether I have six months or one year left—how do I want to spend it?

The answer was clear. I did not desire to travel. I did not want to live in a big house, to have a new car, to represent clients in legal matters, or to behave like a man having a mid life crisis. None of that mattered. What I wanted was to strengthen my relationships with my family, enjoy intimacy with Jesus, participate in people's lives that were being transformed, and to leave a legacy for my family.

How about you? I think it's a question we would each benefit from having been asked, thought about, and answered, "If you had six months left to live, how would you want to spend it?"

How do you find meaning and purpose in life?

About the Author

Peter is an attorney and inspirational speaker. He is currently the Ministry Leader for Celebrate Recovery® and Cancer Support at Walnut Hill Community Church, Bethel, Connecticut. Peter is the proud father of six children: the eldest is 31 years of age and the youngest is 15. He currently lives in Brookfield, Connecticut.

Peter has a passion for sharing his struggles and his life passions as he continues his life journey.

CPSIA information can be obtained
at www.ICGtesting.com
Printed in the USA
LVHW050007211119
637826LV00011B/531/P

9 781087 806204